The Temptation of the West

André Malraux

The Temptation
of the West

*Translated
and with an Introduction
by Robert Hollander*

With a new Preface by
Jonathan D. Spence

The University of Chicago Press
Chicago and London

Originally published in French under the title *La Tentation de l'Occident.*
Copyright, 1926, by Bernard Grasset.

Translation, Introduction and Bibliography Copyright © 1961 by Random House, Inc. Copyright renewed 1989 by Random House, Inc. Published by arrangement with Vintage Books, Random House, Inc.

The University of Chicago Press, Chicago 60637
The University of Chicago Press, Ltd., London

Preface © 1992 by The University of Chicago
All rights reserved. University of Chicago Press edition, 1992
Printed in the United States of America

99 98 97 96 95 94 93 92   6 5 4 3 2 1

Malraux, André, 1901–1976.
   [Tentation de l'Occident. English]
   The temptation of the West / translated and with an introduction by Robert Hollander ; with a new preface by Jonathan D. Spence.
      p.   cm.
   Translation of: La tentation de l'Occident.
   Reprint. Originally published: New York : Vintage Books, 1961.
   ISBN 0-226-50291-0
   1. East and West.   2. China—Civilization.   3. Europe—Civilization.   I. Title.
CB251.M313   1992
303.48'25104—dc20   91-29981
                                                                     CIP

∞The paper used in this publication meets the minimum requirements of the American National Standard for Information Sciences—Permanence of Paper for Printed Library Materials, ANSI Z39.48-1984

Preface

by Jonathan D. Spence

In his opening paragraph to *The Temptation of the West,* André Malraux gives us all the clues we need to get our bearings in this short but dense novel: The book is to be a reverie, dreamed to the throb of engines. To underline this double image, the ship on which Malraux's protagonist "A. D." has embarked for the East is called the *Chambord;* thus, to the "regular pulsing" of the motors, symbol of Western power, is added the evocation of France's days of royal grandeur. For Chambord, the magnificent early sixteenth-century hunting château of King Francis I, was not only an architectural triumph but also something more, a vivid demonstration of the late Renaissance mastery in combining the flamboyant and the geometrical. The reveries, in the same paragraph, artfully run the entire gamut of the stereotypes that the West ascribed in Malraux's time to the "Orient," from "horn-shaped fruits" and palm-framed domes to the restless, frightening armies of the central Asian hordes.

Just as there can be no engines without some distant factories where the components are machined and assembled, so the reveries themselves do not arise spontaneously, with no outside help. Malraux wants his readers to be clear on that point: "Man, capturing living forms one by one and locking them up in books, has prepared the present condition of my mind" (p. 3). By evoking these unnamed precursors, therefore, Malraux is placing his French narrator "A. D." in a cultural context that is narrower than the entire Christian era implied by his name, but still vast. Nineteenth-century France had been awash with reveries of the Middle Eastern "Orient," carried in memoirs, novels, poems, and paintings. By the time Malraux was writing *The Temptation of the West,* in his and the century's early twenties, these Oriental images had been joined (and in some cases edged aside out of the public mind) by new images drawn from China. China, after the Boxer Uprising of 1900 brought avenging Western troops into the heart of Peking, and, especially after 1912 when the last Manchu emperor of the Qing dynasty abdicated, had now become a more open world to the West, one that could be explored with the alleged precision of personal scrutiny.

Because of his passionate concern with the social and political upheavals of the 1920s, 1930s, and 1940s—whether in Vietnam, China, Spain, or in World War II France—analyses of Malraux often push him forward and ahead of himself in both time and percipience. But in the case of *The Temptation of the West,* written while Malraux was still both young and naive, it is surely more helpful to lodge Malraux's view of China amongst those of his immediate literary predecessors, rather than to see him as a revolutionary visionary.

To my mind, the style and emotions of *The Temptation* seem to be indebted particularly to three of Malraux's older contemporaries, Pierre Loti, Paul Claudel, and Victor Segalen. All three of these men were prolific and popular writers who spent considerable periods of time in China. And all three were men who lived in the hectic day-to-day world of politics and practical life—as Malraux was later to do—as well as in the dreamy terrains of their personal Chinas. Pierre "Loti" (Julien

Viaud, 1850–1923) was a marine officer in the French armed forces who saw active duty in China; Paul Claudel (1868–1955) was a diplomat who spent much of the years between 1896 and 1905 stationed as French consul in Fujian; and Victor Segalen (1878–1919) was a physician in the French navy who lived in China for much of the time between 1906 and 1914.

Pierre Loti's *Les Derniers Jours de Pekin* was one of the most successful books published in early twentieth-century France, going through fifty printings between 1902 and 1914. The book grew from pieces Loti wrote for the French newspaper *Figaro* while serving with the French anti-Boxer expeditionary force in 1900 and 1901; and its format is, on the surface, a conventional enough example of the adventure-memoir. But Loti also brought to his reflections an emotional intensity that transforms his book at times into a downbeat hymn to Chinese exoticism.

To give just two examples, for Loti it was not enough for the city wall of Peking to just be itself, it had to evoke a mood that stood for China as a whole. Thus on its first appearance the wall is described as being "the color of mourning, of a height I had never seen before." It "extended without end, in a solitude that was both naked and gray, like some accursed steppe. It seemed like some extraordinary scene-change, carried out with no mechanical sound, no noise from the orchestra, in a silence that was more imposing than any music" (Paris, Calmann-Levy, 1914 ed., pp. 91–92; my translation). Lodged, later, in a billet within an old Chinese mansion, where French troops were quartered after the post-Boxer flight of the Qing court, Loti had a second and more sinister experience. As he lay on the huge bed in his ghostly chamber, without touching the elegant post-party supper that servants had laid out for him, he saw the sharp faces

viii   *Preface*

and gleaming eyes of rats all around him in the palace walls and ceiling. And long after he had extinguished his light, he could hear the chinking of the porcelain plates as the rats jostled each other in their race to consume his untasted patisserie (p. 406).

What Loti sought to pass on to his French readers in *Les Derniers Jours* was the sense of loss that came from knowing too much about China, from having penetrated too deeply into a hitherto forbidden terrain, now powerless to resist the assaults of a Western sensibility. Something similar can be found in the works of Paul Claudel, though Claudel presented his view of turn-of-the-century China without recourse to any overt narrative line. Instead he focused on the images themselves in a series of prose poems through which the Westerner strolls, agape and sometimes aghast, drinking in the sights and smells. Claudel can often serve as a detailed backdrop to the terser phrases of Malraux. Thus, where Malraux refers without precision, in the first of the letters into which *The Temptation* is divided, to the odors which "disgusted" his shore-strolling passengers, who nevertheless remained "pleased and restless," Claudel provides all the specificity of the experienced night-prowler: to him, the smells of a Chinese town are "as strong as an explosive: one smells cooking oil, garlic, animal fact, ashes, opium, urine, excrement, offal" (*Connaissance de l'Est*, 4ème ed. Mercure de France, 1913, p. 28; my translation).

Like Loti with his wall and his rats, Claudel builds his edifice of words from the fleeting Chinese moment. But he goes further than Loti in edging into a world of universal literary discourse, as Malraux was later to do with his fictional creation Ling. Here is Claudel's invocation of a religious text in a Confucian temple:

Here writing possesses this mystery: it speaks. No mo-

ment marks its duration, no position. It is the commence-
ment of an ageless sign. No mouth offers it. It exists; and
the worshiper, face to face with it, ponders the written
name. Solemnly enunciated in the gloom of the shadowy
gold of the baldachin, the sign, between the two columns which are covered with mystic windings of the
dragon, symbolizes its own silence. (*The East I Know*,
Yale University Press, 1914, pp. 45–46)

Loti and Claudel could both write with romantic force
about the China they experienced or dreamed up. But for
the most sensual and violent images of China surely none
of Malraux's contemporaries could match Victor Segalen,
who had published his astonishing poetry cycle *Stèles* in
1912, when he was still only twenty-four. Amongst these
poems, numinous and barbaric, one can find the deepest
echoes for many of Malraux's images, whether of rogue
warriors or of beautiful women. Here one poem from
"The Steles Facing West," in its raw and sensual energy,
must stand as evidence for the rest of Segalen's power:

At Sword Point

We horsemen astride our horses, what do we know
about sowing? But any field that can be
plowed by horse hooves, any meadow that
can be galloped across,
We have trampled.

We do not stoop to build walls or temples,
but any town that will burn, with its temples
and walls,
We have burnt down.

We honor and cherish our women who are all of
high rank; but the others, those who can
be tumbled, spread apart and possessed,
We have taken.

> Our seal is a spearhead; our ceremonial dress,
>   armor starred with dew, our silk is woven
>   from manes. The other kind, which is softer
>   and fetches a price,
>   We have sold.

("At Sword Point," from Victor Segalen, *Stèles,* trans. Michael Taylor. San Francisco, Lapis Press, 1987, no pagination)

If in *The Temptation of the West* Malraux's A. D. placed himself, by firm implication, within such a context of Western absorption with China, then Ling, his Chinese other half, firmly rejected both that Western present and the past that the West built on. Among its various meanings "Ling" in Chinese can be used for "zero," though we cannot be sure that Malraux knew this, or would have cared if he had known. In any case Ling, by rejecting as transitory A. D.'s minor attempts to construct a "moderate nihilism" (p. 98), does not seem to reject nihilism itself. For Ling is a man on the edge of despair, and his assaults on Western compromise, or on its allegedly triumphant assertiveness, are equally damning. He admits to no more than a "hostile curiosity" for Europe (p. 9), and is dejected by the "carefully regulated barbarity" of Europe that blurs the lines separating out civilization from law (p. 13). "Antipathy" is his main emotion when confronted by Western passions (p. 39). Great art, to Ling, is not the "unfortunate assemblage" that he finds hanging on the walls of the Louvre. Such museums "afford me no pleasure" he tells A. D., for the masters of the past are merely "closeted" there, weary proof that Westerners consistently "prefer the satisfaction of critical judgment to the finer joy of understanding" (p. 65). When there is a Western impact in China, as in the cities of the South, Ling sees it as a sad and shallow one: "The cinema, electricity, mirrors, phonographs, all have seduced us like new breeds of domestic animals. For the people of the cities, Europe will forever be only a mechanized fairyland" (p. 110).

On the surface, Ling's thoughts dominate *The Temptation of the West*. He writes twice as many letters as A. D. (twelve to A. D.'s six), and is always more formal than A. D., responding to each of A. D.'s fraternal "Mon cher ami" greetings with the cool "Cher monsieur." But are we not aware, at all times, that it is A. D. setting the pace of the exchanges, and pressuring Ling to respond even when Ling is unsure that he wants to? A. D., too, has both the first and the last word in the novel. And while Ling, after a single letter from Marseilles, settles predictably in Paris, A. D. is either on shipboard or unplaced (as in letters 8 and 12) before finally embarking on an agenda and an itinerary that take him through the great cities of China on a northward journey (Canton to Shanghai to Tientsin)—an itinerary that implies a purpose, even if that purpose is not made completely clear.

In their protracted debates on aesthetics, history, culture, and the sexes, A. D. and Ling move out of the protective shelter of contemporary images and reevoke an earlier literary tradition that had seen its peak in the eighteenth century. The heart of this tradition had been the use of images ostensibly drawn from the Orient as a mode for criticizing the shortcomings of the West. By placing the most complex (and even politically dangerous) questions in the mouth of an apparently naive but shrewd Oriental interlocutor, the Western authors could say the unsayable in comparative freedom. Montesquieu's *Lettres persanes* from 1721 was the most famous French example of this genre, though Montesquieu himself was drawing in his *Lettres* on a rich group of earlier works developing the same idea. But the most powerful of the eighteenth-century fictional dialogues—in literary style, in apparent verisimilitude, and in sophistication of argument—was undoubtedly the Irishman Oliver Goldsmith's *The Citizen of the World,* first published in 1762.

Goldsmith's "Chinese" narrator, Lien Chi Altangi, is presented as an amused and occasionally startled skeptic, peering at English religion and politics with the same bemused concentration that he devotes to the prostitutes and fops in London's public gardens. In Goldsmith's structure, Lien Chi did not have a specific English acquaintance to act as his sounding board. His reflections were relayed instead to an old friend in China, so that the cultural distance was heightened by geographical distance and by time of transmission. Malraux too remained generally vague about the time lapse in the correspondence between A. D. and Ling, so that when a specific indication is given—as in letter 14, for example, when A. D. suddenly mentions that he has been almost two years in China already—the reader is startled and encouraged to reperuse the letter for evidence that A. D. has used this time to deepen his insights into China. This same temporal indicator could also alert the reader, had he or she the energy, to the fact that Ling must have been in Paris for the same length of time. The two friends' overlapping views on the "absurdity" of both fate and their own experiences thus seem more poignant than they did when springing from unfamiliarity with their new environments.

In Malraux's own time, the most debated reprise of Montesquieu's and Goldsmith's "Oriental" reflections were the eight *Letters from a Chinese Official, Being an Eastern View of Western Civilization,* published in London in 1901 and New York in 1903. Though the English scholar Goldsworthy Lowes Dickinson later admitted to being the author, at the time many readers took the letters at their documentary face value, and William Jennings

Bryan was so convinced that the letters were by a Chinese scholar that he published a cross rebuttal in which he tried to defend the values of Christian home and hearth against the sharp Chinese strictures. Dickinson's "Chinese" observer, in words not unlike Ling's just over two decades later, tried to come to grips with the significance of Chinese culture and the nature of its differences from that of the West. As the "Chinese Official" explains it in his second letter:

> Like the prince in the fable, you seem to have released from his prison the genie of competition, only to find that you are unable to control him. Your legislation for the past hundred years is a perpetual and fruitless effort to regulate the disorders of your economic system. Your poor, your drunk, your incompetent, your sick, your aged, ride you like a nightmare. You have dissolved all human and personal ties, and you endeavor, in vain, to replace them by the impersonal activity of the State. The salient characteristic of your civilization is its irresponsibility. You have liberated forces you cannot control; you are caught yourselves in your own levers and cogs. (*Letters from a Chinese Official.* New York, McClure, Phillips & Co., 1903, p. 15)

Malraux's Ling, after a protracted visit to Rome, writes to A. D. of his "disgust" with the city that both promises and yet hides so much. His experience of the Imperial City has left him shaken and perplexed:

> From Hadrian's palace to the second-hand dealers, whose stalls along the Tiber conceal so much mutilated beauty, to the pastry shops, in which decorated mirrors reflect stone symbols of the Will—all join in making this city, from which you have received your law, the very image of chaos. Time, clinging to the stones, amuses itself by bringing their corroded glory to an extreme of Mediterranean picturesqueness. And occasionally, confronted by this too lucid

play of a Western and whimsical time, I mingled my memories of Rome with those of Alexandria: luxury and vulgarity,
idols in the morning sun and violent white crowds in immense squares (p. 26).

Ling's vision of this chaos—at once "European" and
"Oriental"—reads like an extension of ideas that Dickinson had also explored, though Dickinson chose to
present them in the form of his Chinese official's reflections on Jesus, and on the values later espoused in Jesus'
name:

> Enunciated, centuries ago, by a mild Oriental enthusi-
> ast, unlettered, untravelled, inexperienced, they are re-
> markable not more for their tender and touching appeal
> to brotherly love than for their aversion or indifference to
> all other elements of human excellence. The subject of
> Augustus and Tiberius lived and died unaware of the
> history and destinies of imperial Rome; the contempo-
> rary of Virgil and of Livy could not read the language in
> which they wrote. Provincial by birth, mechanic by
> trade, by temperament a poet and a mystic, he enjoyed
> in the course of his brief life few opportunities, and he
> evinced little inclination, to become acquainted with the
> rudiments of the science whose end is the prosperity of
> the State. (*Letters from a Chinese Official,* p. 57)

At the end of his seventh letter, Dickinson's Chinese
official wrote that he claimed no special prowess for himself or his countrymen: "Here are no superhuman vir-
tues, no abnegation of self, no fanatic repudiation of fun-
damental facts of human nature. But here is a life
according to a rational ideal; and here is a belief in that
ideal so effective and profound that it has gone far to
supersede the use of force" (*Letters from a Chinese Official,* p. 64). These are among the central thoughts that
Malraux's Ling tries to hold onto as he probes the West
for its weaknesses and seeks to reassert some confidence

in the deeper levels of China's own civilization. It is one of the most ingenious touches in Malraux's novel that Ling's hope is undercut not so much by A. D. as by a Chinese ex-politician named Wang-Loh, whom A. D. meets in Shanghai. In the long conversation, in letter 16, that A. D. records for his friend Ling, the tired and subtle Wang-Loh attacks the modernizing world of the May 4, 1919, student radicals in China as a world of "idiots intoxicated on university nonsense" (p. 101) who had inherited "a revolution made by sick children" (p. 105). Wang-Loh seems at first to echo Ling's ideas on the West when he tells A. D. that China's "best minds" are now "simultaneously won over, yet disgusted by Europe" (p. 102). China was caught up in a "Theatre of Anguish," says Wang-Loh, an anguish sprung not so much from Western threats or internal warfare as from the Confucian structures that once sheltered and enriched her. "Chinese sensibility" had been a "work of art." Now it was vanishing unmourned:

Those of us who are worthy of China's past are disappearing one by one. Not one understands any more . . . Our tragedy is not in the bloody comedians who lead us, nor even in the constellation of death we see every night. If the Empire, with its russet plains, writhes like a wounded beast, what importance have these games of history? (p. 103).

In letter 17, which serves as the climax of Malraux's novel, Ling in Paris shows how deeply he has been affected by Wang-Loh's words as relayed by A. D. Walking through the Paris streets, amidst the "calm noises of the city" lit by an early evening sun, Ling is overcome by the knowledge "that China is going to die" (p. 109). In a reprise to his earlier sharp and hostile remarks on the Louvre, Ling sees that North China has become a "great, bloody museum," "returned to deeds of green bronze" (p. 109), while South and Central China live in the superficial newness of a purposeless "revolution." The youth now falsely revered as China's new leaders were busy smashing what remained of their civilization "just as the inexperience of young sailors smashes the sculptured prows of junks" (p. 110).

It is never safe, and often folly, to call any writing "prophetic," but the closing two pages of this last letter of Ling's read now as if they had been designed as an epilogue and benediction to the hopes and fears of China's long revolution, and to the millions who died for the future, whether in the anti-Rightist campaigns, the Great Leap Forward, the Cultural Revolution, or under the bullets and tank treads of the People's Liberation Army in June 1989. "What can I tell you?" Ling asks A. D. and us, as he closes. Only that we live in the midst of a "hopeless contradiction," between our acts and our inner lives, answers A. D. on our behalf, a contradiction for which we can say little save that it "prepares us for the metallic realms of the absurd" (p. 118). Separated from the meaning of the inner life, the mind now can only "revolve emptily" like a "beautiful machine soiled by blood-stains" (p. 120).

Is this soiled machine the great ship *Chambord,* we may well ask Malraux, which carried us once with all our reveries across the seas to China? As he has throughout the novel, Malraux answers elliptically: "Always, when the day ended, men thought they saw rich prizes in the darkness." Yet when they reached out for them, they found in their hands "only the last reflections of the dying daylight" (p. 120). It is up to us to decide what to do with this thread of insight as we sail on our way. In the last paragraphs of his novel, Malraux gives us three images from the sea that seem to reinforce the ambiguities we have found in the *Chambord*'s once proud progress. First, the horizon before us now is "naked." Second, even the shore we have left behind shares our melancholy: "From the distance, in the port, a siren howls like a dog off its leash." And, in the closing lines of all, "the yellow wind cries, as in all those foreign nights when the wide wind echoed around me the proud outcry of the sterile sea" (pp. 121–22).

Introduction

by Robert Hollander

André Malraux was born November 3, 1901, in Paris. He is currently *Ministre d'État, chargé des affaires culturelles,* in the cabinet of Charles de Gaulle. Our knowledge of the facts and dates of most of the rest of his adventurous life is a great deal less definite. His youthful study of art in Paris, his trip to Cambodia in search of Khmer art treasures and subsequent mysterious difficulties with the Indochinese authorities, which included a three-year jail sentence, and his ensuing participation in nearly every major world event, from the Chinese Revolution, the Spanish Civil War, the French Resistance, to the Gaullist governments of 1945 and of the present—all have been passed over in comparative silence by Malraux, who is reluctant to make public display of his own activities or thoughts during these vital moments in contemporary history. His unwillingness to become a literary "personality," whether part of an intentionally mysterious pose or not, lends inevitable support to those who claim that his works are their own authorization, that they should not be read as allegorical steps in the journey of Malraux's soul, a quintessence which might then be defined by unifying and handy catchwords. Many of these have been proposed. Depending on which gloss the reader pleases to find definitive, Malraux is a Communist, an Existentialist, a neo-Fascist at heart, an aesthete who has turned his back on reality, an unofficial Catholic. It is enough to say that characters answering all the above descriptions may be found in Malraux's novels.

In a career that has been filled with activity, partisanship, and concern for the practical aspects of the human condition, André Malraux has remained at all times an intellectual. To those who have been able to choose a side and stick to it, Malraux's tendency to formulate one position at a given moment in history, another at a later date, is opportunism. To others it is a sign of his awareness that, in fact, reality itself is always changing. This continuing attempt to define our civilization, which begins with *The Temptation of the West,* is characteristic of Malraux's work. In this sense Malraux is primarily a critic, one who has set for himself the task of revaluating Western civilization.

In 1923 André Malraux set out for Indochina. Except for the few months at the close of 1924 during which he was back in France, he was in turbulent Asia until 1927. His experiences gave him material for his first novels. *The Conquerors, The Royal Way,* and *Man's Fate* are all concerned with Europeans who are directly involved with revolutions in the Orient.

On the other hand, by 1921 Malraux had composed several surrealist *contes.* Previous writers on Malraux have pointed out the presence, behind the frivolous surface of these short works, of the basic plot of all his early fiction—the quest doomed to frustration by its own absurdity. One of these tales, *Royaume-farfelu,* begun in 1920, touched up in 1927, first published in 1928, opens with an Oriental phantasmagoria strikingly similar to the one encountered in A.D.'s first letter in *The Temptation of the West.* But if this letter, written before A.D. has landed in Asia, is surrealistic in tone, it represents applied surrealism, marking a transition from the world of pure fantasy to the even more fantastic "metallic realms of the absurd" that become the eventual vision of all Malraux's early heroes. By the end of the book A.D., twenty-five years old (Malraux's age at the date of Grasset's publication of the work in 1926), has had contact with that nascent China, convulsed by its attempt to define itself, which Malraux uses for the background of *Man's Fate* in 1933. The last five letters of the book display the atmosphere and tone typical of the conversations between the characters in the novels, who are, like Ling and A.D., agonized by their discovery of the meaninglessness that lies at the core of their lives and of their civilizations. In the course of writing *The Temptation of the West,* Malraux seems to have developed his sense of the absurdity of the real world, an absurdity that dwarfs the mere foolishness of most surrealist dreams. Indeed, *The Temptation of the West* announces many of the themes that are prominent in the works that follow. (It is worth noting that not until *The Walnut Trees of the Altenburg* does Malraux allow his characters to spend as much time discussing art as he allows A.D. and Ling to do, although art is an important topic in *Man's Fate* and *Man's Hope.* If his last novel represents a transition to his recent studies of art,

The Temptation of the West is an early indication of Malraux's continuous interest in this field.)

Although rarely discussed as such, *The Temptation of the West* is Malraux's first novel. He himself so classified it by including it in the 1951 Gallimard collection of his novels. And the use of fictive letters as the narrative technique for a novel does not, of course, originate with Malraux. Although most readers will consider this work as a series of philosophical letters rather than as an epistolary novel, it is informative to recall Malraux's admiration for Choderlos de Laclos' *Dangerous Acquaintances,* the most famous French work in this form. Furthermore, A.D. and Ling are not merely ideological spigots for their author. Perhaps they are not E. M. Forster's "round" characters; they are (as Malraux's fictional editor's "Foreword" claims) individuals, and they are fictional; their letters are devices of fiction, even those that seem most philosophical and dogmatic. Like characters in a Chekhov play who never stop talking long enough to listen, A.D. and Ling at times address their impassioned messages to one who replies without seeming to have heard.

The Temptation of the West, whatever its technical qualifications as a novel, also reflects Malraux's interest in philosophy, especially in Nietzsche. In Nietzsche, with his analyses of Western decadence, Malraux found an exalted precursor, more important for showing the way toward developing cultural generalizations than for shaping specific concepts. For Malraux's book is consciously a product of the first quarter of the new century, when, if God was dead, as Nietzsche had declared, Nietzsche was dead also. The letters, after attempting to analyze the world's intellectual and emotional predicament, end with an uncertain glance at the future.

This book, in addition to being Malraux's first important published work, is also important in the literary history of our century. And, if being topical is a literary virtue, *The Temptation of the West* should be especially interesting today. For we cannot fail to be struck by this apparently prophetic vision of a China which thirty-five years of history have translated into one of the great forces in our time.

A few notes are necessary. First, in all three French editions of the text the date line of the twelfth letter, written by A.D., reads "Paris." M. Malraux, in a most helpful note to the translator, has instructed that there should be no date line at this point, that A.D. was then on his way to Canton. The translator has emended the text in accordance with this information.

Second, the meaning of the title is manifold, although its various significations eventually merge. "Temptation" generally means either "enticement" or "trial." Europe clearly offers A.D. little enticement. But from Ling we understand that European values are attractive to the inhabitants of his country, that the West "tempts" the East. We are also aware that A.D. seeks from the Orient that which he finds lacking at home.

Of course the plain and most significant intention of the title is to be found in Letter 12, p. 78, when A.D. announces: "This great, troubled drama which is beginning, dear friend, is one of the temptations of the West." Yet then we must also acknowledge that young Chinese, in desiring to be rid of their traditions, in responding to the allurements of European culture, suffer precisely the same state of temptation which their Occidental counterparts endure. Indeed, each of these men feels that he and his civilization are undergoing crucial tests, and each of them finally senses that there is no civilization that can withstand its own disintegration, its ultimate and hopeless test.

Last, the translator wishes to express his gratitude to all who helped him by being generous with their time, their judgment and their knowledge. The imperfections in this rendering are, however, his own responsibility.

COLUMBIA UNIVERSITY
May 5, 1961

A Selective Bibliography

of the works of André Malraux and of
translations currently in print.

Lunes en papier. Paris: Editions des Galeries Simon, 1921.

La Tentation de l'Occident. Paris: B. Grasset, 1926.
The Temptation of the West. Translated by Robert Hollander (1961). University of Chicago paperback, 1992.

Les Conquérants. Paris: B. Grasset, 1928.
The Conquerors. Translated by Stephen Becker (1976). New York: Holt, Rinehart and Winston. University of Chicago Press paperback, 1992.

Royaume-farfelu. Paris: Gallimard, 1928.

La Voie royale. Paris: B. Grasset, 1930.

La Condition humaine. Paris: Gallimard, 1933.
Man's Fate. Translated by Haakon Chevalier (1934). New York: Random House, 1990.

Le Temps du mépris. Paris: Gallimard, 1935.

L'Espoir. Paris: Gallimard, 1937.
Man's Hope. Translated by Stuart Gilbert and Alastair Macdonald. New York: Random House, 1984.

La Lutte avec l'ange, I: Les Noyers de l'Altenburg. Lausanne, Yverdon: Editions du Haut Pays, 1943.
The Walnut Trees of Altenburg. Translated by A. W. Fielding. London: J. Lehmann, 1952. University of Chicago Press paperback, 1992.

Oeuvres complètes. (I. *La Condition humaine.* II. *Le Temps du mépris.* III. *L'Espoir.* IV. *Les Conquérants.* V. *La Tentation de l'Occident. Royaume-farfelu. Lunes en papier.* VI. *La Lutte avec l'ange, I.* VII. *La Voie royale.*) Genève: Skira, 1945.

Romans. (*Les Conquérants, La Condition humaine, L'Espoir.*) Paris: Gallimard (Bibliothèque de la Pléiade), 1947.

The Case for De Gaulle; a Dialogue between André Malraux and James Burnham. Section by Malraux translated by Spencer Byard. New York: Random House, 1948.

Romans. (*La Tentation de l'Occident, Les Conquérants, La Voie royale, La Condition humaine, Le Temps du mépris, L'Espoir, Les Noyers de l'Altenburg.*) Paris: Gallimard, 1951.

Saturne. Paris: Gallimard, 1950.

La Psychologie de l'art. (I. *La Musée imaginaire.* II. *La Création artistique.* III. *La Monnaie de l'absolu.*) Genève: Skira, 1947, 1949, 1950.

Les Voix du silence. Paris: Gallimard, 1951.

> *The Voices of Silence.* Translated by Stuart Gilbert. Bollingen Series Vol. XXIV. Princeton University Press paperback, 1978.

La Métamorphose des dieux. Paris. Gallimard, 1957.

Antimémoires. Paris: Gallimard, 1967.

> *Anti-Memoirs.* Translated by Terence Kilmartin (1968). Henry Holt paperback, 1990.

Les Chênes qu'on abat. Paris: Gallimard, 1971.

La Tête d'obsidienne. Paris: Gallimard, 1974.

Lazare. Paris, Gallimard, 1974.

> *Lazarus.* Translated by Terence Kilmartin. Grove-Weidenfield, 1978.

Les Hôtes de Passage. Paris: Gallimard, 1975.

Etre et Dire. Paris: Gallimard, 1978.

The Temptation of the West

A vous, Clara, en souvenir
du temple de Banteaï-Srey.

Foreword

The letters which make up the greater part of this book were written by Messrs. A.D., French, twenty-five years old, possessing some knowledge of Chinese art, and Ling-W.-Y., Chinese, twenty-three, drawn to the West's different and uniquely bookish culture, a culture which infects many of his countrymen. The former in China, the latter in Europe, they exchanged these letters during the course of their travels.

Let no one find in Mr. Ling a symbol of the Far East. Such a symbol could not possibly exist. He is Chinese and, as such, dominated by Chinese sensibility and thought, which not even the books of Europe are able to destroy.

No more.

These letters have been selected and edited. By publishing them, we propose to delineate the developments of two sensibilities, and to suggest to those who read them some arresting thoughts on the seemingly unusual sensuous and spiritual lives of these two men.

1

A. D. writes:

. . . .

How often have I seen savages suddenly appear and offer seafarers horn-shaped fruits from primitive trays, while cupolas gleam through the palms! Discoveries! . . . Man, capturing living forms one by one and locking them up in books, has prepared the present condition of my mind. A procession of beings and landscapes is unfolding tonight in my thoughts. Mingled with them, the regular pulsing of the engines seems to be a part of this dark, watery silence. Supreme calm; the polished sparkling sea where the deep stars tremble . . . In the ship's wake the last hordes disappear, rearing their huge oxen skulls —standards or trophies?—their curved shadows streaking the level plains. Further on, the armies of Central Asia are in turbulence. Tall banners, ornamented with ancient, black characters, dominate everything. Long ago.

In the depths of the harem, the concubines. In an archway one of them (soon to be the favorite) gossips with a eunuch, whose eyes are closed. In his violet palace, the Emperor examines the fossils gathered for him from all his domain. It is cold.

Outside, frozen cicadas come loose from branches, striking the ground with the sound of pebbles. In the center of a square, evil magicians are being burned at an odoriferous stake; the figurines of hollow wood, which they had used to cast spells on princesses, explode and shoot up like fireworks. The crowd—so many blind men!—falls back quickly. Near the horizon, in the wild grass, a line of ant-covered bones marks the path of armies. Not far from the fire, the magicians' widows have seen the future.

Some foxes hurry by.

Each spring the Tartar roses, white with purple hearts, cover the Mongolian steppes. There caravans pass; dirty merchants lead tall, shaggy camels, loaded down with round packages which burst open like pomegranates when the caravan halts. Then all the enchantment of this snowy kingdom—stones the color of clear sky or frozen stream, stones that glitter like ice, the pale plumage of gray birds, frost-colored furs, and silver-stamped turquoises—pours out into the merchants' agile fingers.

From the height of flat-roofed Tibetan monasteries an exquisite mystery descends, down along roads padded with sand to the very edge of the sea; there it spreads itself out in numberless, extravagant temples, studded with trembling bells.

The men of my race arrive on wingless, eyeless ships.

They enter the harbors with the dawn. The milky water, reflectionless, makes the first cries of the bargemen more distinct; above the lacquered bay the whole city, its crown of ramparts jeweled with pagodas, rouses itself in the sun; all along its sharp profile appear plumes and tassels of light. The men reach the shore; a few stones are hurled at them; then they wander, pleased and restless, into streets whose odor disgusts them, pursued by the chime of the silver pieces that money-changers put to the test with delicate hammers. Sometimes they catch a glimpse of a woman; when the curtain is drawn again, they try to remember her composed features and exceedingly small feet, her silk trousers and patterned bodice, try to remember the room of black wood, russet shadow and twisted flowers . . .

They visit the official pawnshops, towers slotted with loopholes; next to each loophole is a small basin filled with acid, which the guards hurl down on the bandits who try to steal treasures of the State.

Then they return, terribly shaken about in heavy chairs, their purchases piled high on their stomachs. That white satin robe was once the funeral gown of a young princess of the islands, who was draped in it on the day of her death, a red jewel between her lips. In peaceful, sunlit courtyards old men make magical gestures, describing the buildings of distant cities in Turkestan or Tibet, while grave adolescents look on. In the pet shops parrots speak complicated tongues, learned long ago from the wise men of forty thousand foreign islands.

Guided by Lascars (Levantines who belong to secret societies), white adventurers, after learning Manchurian and shaving off their eyebrows, have reached the interior; there they have married Manchurian women and now, important generals, command the Imperial armies. They have no desire to acknowledge old friends; those who go to visit them are put to death at their command. Further north, cunning and all-powerful, alone in the depths of the most solemn palace of the forbidden city, the Emperor spreads his thin, transparent hand over China, land of work, opium and dreams, blind old man crowned with black poppies . . . And there are those older ghosts, martial and wise, of the T'ang emperors; the tumult of the courts where every religious and magical system of the world came into conflict; Taoist thinkers; queens fastened to walls by rough arrows; warriors, their weapons embellished with horsetails; generals dead under tents, lost in the North after sixty victories; tombs, in the middle of the wilderness, guarded only by soldiers and horses graven on broken slabs; mournful chants; armies with their parallel ranks of spears, their animal skins, moving across the vast, sterile lands in the frozen night. But what can I recover from your hollow surge of victories, O vestiges?

2

Ling to A. D.

Cher Monsieur,

Europe calls forth few beautiful ghosts, and I have come to her with hostile curiosity. The illusions which she has created in us Chinese are too indefinite for us to find instruction or pleasure in modifying them: the influence of books and of our own anguish has made us investigate the thought of Europe rather than her forms. Her present attracts us more than the broken frame of her past, from which we seek only enlightenment as to the source of her strength.

Her name evokes neither specific scenes nor a longing for them. The photographs I saw in China failed to express that movement in a crowd peculiar to the West; I had preconceived a continent swallowed whole by geometry: roofs of buildings and streets made straight lines; clothing was rigid, furniture rectangular. Palace gardens proved—not unbeautifully—theorems. An unceasing creation, renewed by action in a world destined to act—that is what then seemed to me the soul of Europe, where all was subordinate to man's will. The Chinese junk, a domestic animal, seemed to me transformed, in the French sailboat, into an ingenious harmony of triangles. Moreover, Europe was for me the only place in the world where Woman existed.

3

Ling to A. D.

Cher Monsieur,

I should like to add a few words to my last letter. I'm beginning to recognize the value that cultivated Frenchmen (so different from those we see in China) attach to sincerity, and that encourages me. Furthermore, several weeks here have given my impressions some sharpness. I perceive in Europe a carefully regulated barbarity, in which the concepts of civilization and of law are each day confused. Civilization is not a social, but a psychological, phenomenon; true civilization must be based on emotion.

What then shall I say about these men of your race? I study them; I try very hard to escape from books. I know that our translators, in their effort to make known to us the manners and morals of Europe as well as her literature, by selecting Balzac, Flaubert, the French naturalists, the early novels of Goethe, the works of Tolstoy and Dostoievski, by analyzing the genius of Baudelaire, have shown wisdom and great care. But aren't these exceptional, even almost insane Christians, who scream and weep with anguish, from Emma Bovary to the brothers Karamazov? Nevertheless . . .

What an impression of sadness I get from your public entertainments, from all the miserable creatures I notice in the streets! Your dedication to action shocks me less than those grief-stricken faces I can't escape. Grief seems to battle, hand to hand, with each of you. So much *individual* suffering!

At one time your religion had the universe in its sway, and, whatever antipathy it awakes in me, I can only contemplate with respect the almost barbaric images it produced of itself, in which is frozen a great, harmonious suffering. But I couldn't possibly imagine, without great difficulty, meditations in which all the intensity of love is concentrated on a lacerated body. And to me it seems that the Christian religion is responsible for precisely those emotions which give rise to consciousness of self. I have visited the galleries of your museums; your genius filled me with anguish. Even your gods, their grandeur, as well as their actual images, stained by blood and tears, are animated by a brutal strength. And a tragic destiny weighs on the lowered eyelids of those few peaceful visages that I should like to have loved. But you painted them precisely because you knew they were death's élite.

"There are also our works in voluptuous praise of life." Still more than the others, these oppress me. Don't you understand that in order to take pride in having discovered the female body a man must belong to a race weighed down by the heavy crown of power and anguish?

A work conceived as are those you admire, one which is understood and enjoyed for the same style, charm and cogency by all, is a minor work. It is their ability to evoke in us the infinite diversity of life that constitutes the true value of our most treasured silk scrolls. Moreover, the arts in themselves have little grandeur. What elevates them is that they are elements of a perfect purity which has infinitely varied modes. Those porcelains are there only in order to capture, one by one, the thousand forms of beauty which that dark and silent room obscures. Numberless, unknown, the emotions which have the power to transform us wander over the face of the earth; our hands, joined in a chalice of desire, could not catch them half so well as those ephemeral shapes, so carefully arranged in the shadows . . .

The artist is not the man who creates, but the one who feels. Whatever may be the qualities, or the quality, of a work of art, it is minor, for it is no more than one proposition of beauty. All the arts are decorative. Consider, for example, bamboos, on which the multicolored birds of the imagination love to perch, or banyans, which have the pomp of funeral chants; give the gardener, a man worthy of consideration, his salary and at least some respect. But now look at the river which mirrors these things; it alone is truly worthy of admiration.

Every civilization shapes a sensibility. The great man is neither the painter nor the writer, but rather the man who is capable of carrying this sensibility to its perfection. Refining in themselves the sensibility of their race, and, in expressing it, moving constantly toward a higher pleasure—that is the life of those among us whom you would call "masters."

Greatness, whether yours, that of armed men, of sadness, or ours, that of perfection, arises from the intensity of emotion a feeling wakes in men. For you, it is a sentiment of sacrifice: admiration is reserved for action. For us, it is but the awareness that we exist in accord with the most beautiful mode. The forms of art which you have been accustomed to call sublime express an action rather than a state. This state, of which we know nothing except that it gives, to those who attain it, a sense of purity, of the separateness of the soul in the heart of the eternal light, has never been sought by Occidentals, although the languor offered by certain stretches of the Mediterranean affords them the opportunity to seek it. Thence springs the sole sublime expression of art and of man; it is called serenity.

I should like, Monsieur, to write further concerning the men of Europe; but as yet I have seen only their works.

4

Ling to A. D.

Cher Monsieur,

I observe Europeans; I listen to them; I don't believe they understand what life is. Their imagination must be praised for having invented the devil. But since his ·death, they seem to be prey to a more chaotic divinity: the intellect.

Your minds are of such a nature that they are capable of grasping only the fragmentary elements of life. You are completely carried away by the goals toward which you are incessantly aiming. You desire conquest. What do you find behind your meager victories?

We Chinese try to grasp only the entirety of life. Not that we are able to do this. Still, we know that this entirety is, and must be, greater than any one of our individual acts. Just as, finding among ancient sketches a drawing of an arm, without knowing anything of the person whose arm it actually was, one knows that there was a hand at its end, so do we know and *feel* that beyond every act, whatever its importance, a yet hidden life extends its numberless ramifications. Life is a succession of possibilities from which we secretly desire to select and embellish a few . . . We want to limit our mind to being a spectator at its own game: the unceasing modification of the universe. I know that may sound frivolous to you. But the play of light and shadow, which is all a superior mind can see in the incoherence of the universe, is nonetheless, for me, the only spectacle in which a civilized man can interest himself without shame.

Of course, whatever effort I make, my awareness of a given act is necessarily different from yours. My sensibility struggles against the limitations my mind might try to impose on it. This struggle is not the result of a desire for reality, but is a vice of the sensibility. Merely because it hasn't happened yet, is our future life any less real? As for the importance you attribute to those acts which stagger your imaginations (because you haven't learned how to understand that their importance is attenuated), doesn't it arise from an intelligence which is careless and, perhaps, poorly trained by a religion that never ceases to make you believe in your own, individual existence? You have offered up your lives to power. You confuse yourselves with your actions, even with your thoughts . . . You barely understand that in order to be, it should not be necessary to act, and that the world changes you far more than you change it . . .

Depending upon the insinuations of our sensibility and of the moment, we want to be able to choose between the successive aspects time may give any object we are currently preoccupied with, be it action or thought. It is this constant possibility for change that spreads its multiple and ambiguous sovereignty over China, and gives us the subtle excitement we seek. I wonder if you have yet seen a merchant stake his entire business on a roll of the dice, lose, and change places with his employee, who has won? Then, much later, he will play again, win, and resume his former role! And one can hardly discern the least trace of emotion in his expression. These painful moments in an unknown life cannot be taken to heart, even though one senses how real they are, since fortune may be on the verge of setting them right.

You have weighted the universe with anguish. What a tragic countenance you have given to death! A cemetery in a large European city fills me with unpleasant thoughts. I think of the cemeteries you are doubtless seeing even now, of the fields of the dead, where some silent bird rules over the meditations of friendly graves . . .

From these fields of death, wholly imbued with tenderness, there arise only two emotions for us: sadness and awe. In your popular novels death is the symbol of terror. How distant from you are the green and yellow devils with their numerous jests, the dragons who arch their backs when you caress them, and all the kindly monsters of the funeral procession that trail behind an Oriental death, without ruffling its dignity by their presence!

The European belief that in China death's influence is unceasing is but illusion and folly. That we allow rabbits to perch upon so many graves without a thought of sacrilege reinforces in us a concept of death which has nothing in common with yours. What we feel is a profound tenderness. It is also the awareness of not being limited to oneself, of being the setting for, rather than a means to, action. Each of us honors his own dead, and all the dead, as the symbols of a force that surrounds him, that is one of the modes of existence, although all he can know of that force is that it exists. But we *experience* this existence: it dominates and shapes us without our being able to grasp it. We are filled with it, since we are men, while you are geometers, even of divinity . . . Time is what *you* make it; we are what it makes us.

5

Ling to A. D.

forms that pour it forth in streets where ancient stones are whitened by the sun. The sombre grandeur of her voice was obscured by the singing of fountains, whose charm books had already revealed to me—the passionate rush of your gods and bronze Tritons pervading the sacred city, and each street hiding in its own shadow the sensual shadow of Bernini . . .

The few fragments of ruined walls which dot the fields of Carthage would have disappointed and seduced me less, perhaps, than this union of porticoes and stalls, of fluted columns and shops, than that great square where the ruins of the Forum are extended against a backdrop of Romantic buildings, capped by famous domes. From Hadrian's palace to the second-hand dealers, whose stalls along the Tiber conceal so much mutilated beauty, to the pastry shops, in which decorated mirrors reflect stone symbols of the Will—all join in making this city, from which you have received your law, the very image of chaos. Time, clinging to the stones, amuses itself by bringing their corroded glory to an extreme of Mediterranean picturesqueness. And occasionally, confronted by this too lucid play of a Western and whimsical time, I mingled my memories of Rome with those of Alexandria: luxury and vulgarity, idols in the morning sun and violent white crowds in immense squares. However, near archways stained black-green, near columns forgotten in the middle of tiny unpaved squares where the common people sleep in the shade, or near the great, empty Colosseum, I heard the call of Empire, which so many of your race come to listen to here. As the setting sun, for a few seconds, enamels the uneven sea, that call reunited my scattered thoughts:

"What use to extol power if one is not an emperor? A great empire is beautiful; so is its fall. This city learns to serve in order to rule: a lesson taught by simple soldiers! In the acceptance by an entire race of the ideal which prevails here there is something base and vulgar. For men to bow so low annoys me . . . It is power which should serve, and serve a higher master than a systematic allegory of itself. Whatever weakness I may sense in the flourishes of Timur or of Alexander, those other barbarians, I prefer them to the Imperial shadows which, one after another, bring to this shining river the homage of their controlled courage. If I worshipped order, I should want it to be made for me, not me for it . . ."

I returned, with the sad smile that thoughts like these bring on, through narrow streets where watermelon merchants set up their stalls, thinking about that ironic quality of power which makes the Roman soul vanish entirely, for your race, in the sudden rise of her dominance in a single century, and makes necessary the inclusion of some awkward juxtapositions in a revised estimate of her true strength. "I understand well," I thought further, "what these fragments are telling me: 'He who sacrifices himself joins in the grandeur of the cause to which he sacrifices.' But the only grandeur I can see in this cause is that which it owes to sacrifice. It is without intelligence. The men whom it directs are dedicated to death, whether they give or receive it. Because it is powerful, is barbarism any less barbaric?" And the ruins imposed on my thoughts only their soiled and chaotic nobility . . . O sterile plains of Samarkand, where the presence of one name and two black minarets standing against a clear sky create the highest tragic emotion!

Alas! I wanted to find here that vitality which my race needs so badly, and, in the presence of its most treasured image, Rome, I am unable to hide my disgust . . .

6

Ling to A. D.

Cher Monsieur,

I wish to speak further of Rome. Rome and Athens have been continually present in my thoughts, and, uttering words different from those I had gone to them to hear, force me to listen. The image of them which is reflected by Europe is more vital than the one I carry in my memory. I didn't write you of Athens while I was in that city because of the great uncertainty I was feeling there. I already knew what I wanted to take away; I was only waiting for it to appear. In the new city the charm of the wispish pepper plants hardly moderated my displeasure with the modern monuments. The ancient city, where I had expected to discover a new and Persian purity, and which was for me the symbol of a laureled race, standing high on the walls of a fortress, I found disconcerting; still, perhaps there is no idea among all those I have acquired in the course of this journey that is not attached by at least a slender thread to those broken columns and that firm horizon, that hasn't recalled the little museum on the Acropolis, silent, intimate, where an old Greek soldier pointed out to me a few slabs of stone, the most fitting symbol of the West I have yet seen. He loved them. He patted them like a modest collector. Yet he preferred the olive tree of the goddess, and offered me a branch for a reasonable price. Since there is no eternal beauty, soon more eminent shades are certain to prevail over the procession of these others, which was pure and has become charming. Yet it is fitting that the greatest minds of your race come here, seeking a clear image of what they are. Could more magniloquent homage be offered to the dead than the advent of beautiful, clear souls, hungry to know themselves?

Nevertheless, this harmony is thin, this purity is merely human. A few moments ago, while I was recalling that unassuming museum from among the forms I have discovered while traversing the world, a bust of a young man, eyes open, suddenly confronted me, like an allegory of Greek genius, with this penetrating intimation: measure all things by the duration and intensity of *a single* human life. Beneath this unknown face shouldn't you engrave the name Oedipus? His story is the struggle of all your faculties against the Sphinx. The monster—dragon, sphinx, winged bull—is one of the mirrors of the East; but it belongs also to that part of the soul that Greece tried to conquer, and has reappeared, through the centuries, each time men ask of life more than their minds can give them. Dead in Thebes, it was reborn in Egypt, in Sogdiana, and on the borders of India, where it conquered that mournful Oedipus, Alexander, in his turn . . .

A single human life. To my Asiatic consciousness, all of Greece's genius rests on that single concept and on the sensibility derived from it. Therein resides an act of faith. The Greek saw man set apart from the world, as the Christian sees him bound to God, as we see him bound to the world. For the Greek everything was ordered by its relationship to man. The particular stamp of his gods, the one which characterizes their essence, is not at all that they were human, but that they were personal. We recognized, as he did, man's importance and the perfection of which he is capable. But we conceived the universe in its entirety, and were as aware of the forces which form it as of the vital human elements it contains; in our thought the notion of mankind was quick to conquer that of man. The Greeks thought of man as an individual, a being who is born and dies. The span of life, which has no more importance for our thought and sensibility than its divisions—youth, maturity, old age—have for yours, became for them the major truth of the universe. For the awareness, or what I should call the sensation, of being a particle of the universe, which necessarily precedes the totally abstract notion of man, they substituted the awareness of being a living organism, complete, discrete, on a friendly earth where the only impassioned images were those of men and of the sea. Thus it is a particular sensibility, rather than any actual thought, which comes from those practically bare landscapes to influence your culture. The West was born there, under the austere face of Minerva, bearing its armor as well as the stigmata of its future madness. You claim that the ardor which is rising in us is soon to defeat us; that the one which burns in you is a force for creation. "It is prudent to leave in peace," the sorcerers of my land have said, "the dragons who sleep in the earth . . ." After the death of the Sphinx, Oedipus attacks himself.

Rome, after one has discovered its traces of Hellenism, is no longer an Imperial tomb, but the only place where the greatest compassion is slowly turned into power. Whether an individual proudly exalts or humbly examines himself, the Seven Hills will teach him submission. Could one better understand your civilization and its rhythm than by listening to the dialogues which rise from these two cities, so full of broken marble, their voices respectively eager and proud? It pleased me, in this city of the lictors (whose only genius was employed in fastening the stalks of the *fasces* to the dominating ax), to come upon so many churches whose interior columns are the remains of ancient temples. There I heard two Christian voices: one sang the glory of God; the other questioned it in hollow tones. This second voice was no longer seeking to make men aware of those of his powers—from strength to lust—which affirm his being by making him distinct from the universe; rather, it was to his hesitations, to his regrets, to the internal struggles which constitute his life that this voice accorded supreme intensity and importance, and in them found God. The irresponsible Oriental brings himself to rise above a conflict in which his salvation is not at stake. The Christian *is in no way capable* of separating himself from such a conflict: God and he are indissolubly joined, and the universe is but the vain backdrop for their combat. In the intellectual torment of the Greeks, in the pure uneasiness they encountered in the attempt to give life a human meaning, are found the reflections of your present anguish and your blind man's gestures. God reveals himself to you through violent emotions; it is in ordering these emotions that you reach out toward Him. To reach out . . . For you, God is a state; for us, a rhythm.

7

Ling to A. D.

(in answer to a letter of no importance)

Cher Monsieur,

No, not merely the violent passions, but all passions are nurtured by our popular beliefs. The troubled shapes which, in the evenings, swarm up from the ricefields, hide themselves behind the porcelain fish which ornament the roofs of pagodas, or keep you company, like faithful or mischievous dogs, as you walk along rain-drenched paths, are passions. Born of you, they depart and go around the world to rejoin their numerous and varied sisters. How many of these spirits whisper together above the autumnal earth to make that sound which rises from the mist-filled trees, when heavy drops of water fall singly from the mangoes, saturated with rain! . . .

I cannot be astonished at the weakness of the men of your race when they confront their passions. Their way of conceiving and experiencing time, as well as the idea they have of themselves, drives them to this state. Love interests me more than anything else. I used to enjoy speculating on what a man could become. Today I like doing so even more; for the antipathy I feel toward Europe does not always protect me from her, and I also become eager to sketch my portrait, even if I must finally destroy it. How can

I find myself, except in an examination of your race? I watch you lose yourselves somewhat in love, regretting that I can't follow you; to lose myself, it would first be necessary for me to believe in myself.

It seems to me that you lend too much importance to generally accepted reality. The world created by this acceptance, to which you conform because to deny it would demand too much strength of him who tried, weighs heavy on you. In your social order passion represents a convenient outlet. Whatever our race is, we do accept the fact that we live in a predetermined universe; but a kind of savage joy invades every one of us when the urging of our deeper needs shows us just how unpredictable they are. The passionate man is as out of place in the world he imagines as in the world he experiences; yet even if he could foresee his passion, he would be able to do nothing to change it. The man who wants to love wants to escape, which is little enough; but the man or woman who desires to be loved, who wants another person to be lost in himself, submits, in my opinion, to a necessity so powerful that I can only describe it as containing the following proposition: *at the core of European man, ruling the important movements of his life, is a basic absurdity.* Don't you agree?

I ceased writing some time ago. This idea obsesses me. What is it you wish to possess in what you call the "soul" of women? While they were Christians, women sacrificed their religion; then they sacrificed their judgment. But today the conflict is even more difficult, for it is impossible to sacrifice one's sensibility to an ideal; and so it seems that such concepts are dying out in Europe . . .

I think that the passions you experience are less successful in shaping external reality to their mold than in disorganizing you. They have no effect on "values," but only intensify a thing's existence. Organization is a purely mental phenomenon; that is your problem. And no other one of your passions, as much as love, caresses the beast and then arouses him. When I force myself to distinguish between your torment in love and the torment of conquest, it sometimes seems to me that I am witnessing an anguished search for unity. I don't forget that your religion has taught you to investigate the world only after giving you a heightened awareness of its essential disorder . . .

All this, alas! is merely speculation. Without great advantage to China, I have been making comparisons between our two cultures. These exaggerated impressions, with some reflections on them, follow:

Woman is a worthy enough object of attention, capable, like the work of art, of beauty, and destined to the accomplishment of certain duties. If she is to be a wife, let her be fertile and faithful; if a concubine, beautiful; if a courtesan, well versed in her art. That she be wanton is not at all desirable; it is enough that she be able to care for her husband or supply her lover with pleasantly varied amusements. Our concept of her prevents our giving her any particular personality: How could a young man love a girl whom he has never seen, to whom his parents had affianced him at the age of ten? Our writers have always depicted the passion that a woman can inspire in a man as being outside marriage, for it is worked by magic. Whether he who suffers from it accepts or struggles against such a passion, it is always passive. Like a mortal disease, it is never-ending and hopeless. Neither possession nor even the certainty of reciprocity weakens its hold; it is not at all within men's power to fend off the eternal wounds of destiny . . .

The roles of concubine and courtesan sometimes demand intelligence, always cleverness and care; but any note of individuality would be considered a blemish. We are continually astounded by the sumptuousness of European brothels: there are few respects in which the barbarism Europe has retained strikes us so forcibly; of all his ideas, is there any one more revealing of a man's sensibility than his concept of pleasure? I am not unaware of the fact that it would be ridiculous to judge Europe on the basis of such things; still . . . To be interested in women and desire them only for their beauty is a sign of grossness! In China there is no courtesan of any status who is uncultured, unable to embellish the physical pleasures she bestows upon a man with those of the mind. Reading is always reading; but there are good and bad books, charming embellishments and mediocre ones. A courtesan must be cultured in order that her favors be enjoyable, and ingenious in order to know how to preserve them. And nothing has a less individualistic character than this culture and this ingenuity, which are akin to the techniques of the craftsman. The qualities we seek in a woman are the same as those by which we judge a man charming; the most sought-after courtesan almost always has had to bow down before boys prepared only by twelve or fifteen years of studies . . .

It is evident that you are affected by what a

woman has of the unique about her. How can you understand what disposes you to love one woman and not another? It is not beauty; ugly women are loved. (A woman's beauty may.be a source of pride, but it never offers promise of emotional fulfillment.) The one thing that offers real promise: the expressiveness of the face, body, and voice. These justify all impulsive seductions, even those whose effects wear off little by little once the soul, now familiar, allows the face to speak only of forgotten promises. A woman affects a man by proposing to him the emotions he needs or desires; between sensual pleasure and suffering there are emotions which move almost all of us; others respond only to rare and secret weaknesses, and their effect is even more profound.

The young girls and women of China do not try to set themselves apart by emphasizing individualistic traits. Their coiffeur, their make-up, and the smallness of their eyes all contribute to a similarity, as does, perhaps even more than their appearance, the emptiness of their existence. Only the courtesans of elevated rank and the geishas of Japan are, at times, exceptions.

Therefore, it is they who are the heroines of all our love stories. Ever since women have been admitted to our universities and no longer accept the old traditions, our students have acquired an overwhelming interest in the emotion which you call "love." With sadness they see you confuse it with the accompanying sexual pleasures; your discourses on this subject seem to them uninformed and naïve. It is only that they ignore the priceless effects the imagination has taught you.

Young Chinese who read your books are at first astounded by the pretense you make of understanding the emotions of women. In addition to the fact that such an effort is, in their opinion, worthy of scorn, it is inevitably doomed to failure. Men and women belong to different species. What would you think of an author who set out to reveal the inner thoughts of birds? That he is merely presenting a distortion of his own ideas. That is our opinion of the writer who discusses women in this way. However, from this attempt comes the power of European women. It seems that you take her hand to place it on your shoulder: she interests you because she touches you, but it is you who strive to allow her to touch you. In so far as you attempt to understand her, you assume her identity.

I remember the words of your friend G. E. He had just come from Syria. We were speaking of women, for they had been on my mind constantly for several days. "I was surprised," he told me, "at the sensations they awoke in me in the first Moslem countries I visited. Veiled, they walked with tiny steps in the street, followed by their servants; their shadows advanced slowly along a high wall which cut the sky with a slanting line of red battlements. I was curious to analyze the sensual response aroused in me by the care they take in veiling their faces. I think I felt, in attenuated form, the emotions that I projected into each of them. But these emotions I experienced were modified; they were not theirs, but those of a woman who might understand the emotions of men, those of a man suddenly transformed into a woman . . ." I continually find such a difference between the object and the form, shaped by your sensibility, which it assumes—outlining the forms of the world and escaping thought. The Western concept of love gathers its force and complexity from the necessity you feel to identify yourselves, voluntarily or not, with the woman you love; she is bound to the union it implies in her of tender sympathy and erotic pleasure. But one cannot without a struggle take an ideal for a partner.

I await your answer with great curiosity, and with the regret that there is no word in the French language which expresses this thought without making it seem a bit shabby.

8

A. D. to Ling

Mon cher ami,

The excessive importance we have been led to give to "our" reality is doubtless just one of the means the mind employs to defend itself. For affirmations of that kind bolster us more than they explain anything. Man, who for thousands of years has been seeking within himself his limitations and his reality, is never satisfied until his search has met with failure. He finds himself in the world or in God. The men you have been observing are still seeking within themselves. Beware their words.

By accepting the notion of the subconscious, and by having become fascinated with it, Europe has deprived herself of her best weapons. The absurd, the beautiful absurd, linked with us like the serpent to the tree of Good and Evil, is never completely hidden, and we watch it prepare its most seductive games with the wholehearted assent of our will. If it is possible to judge others on the basis of their actions alone, we can't do the same for ourselves; the real universe, harmonious and controlled, is only that place inhabited by other men. Our own is a dream world, a golden chain of victories. A few moments of solitude and boredom suffice to make

us find again, in ourselves, the distant memory of
shining armor: the highest glory of the dramas of
history and of art is that they are relived each day
in the depths of numberless, obscure conscious-
nesses. For the Western soul is to be found in the
commotion of dreams . . . These games, the absurdity of which would be terrible if it were not
commonplace, leave in us vestiges nearly as strong
as memories. Intellect molds the concept of a nation;
what gives it emotional vitality is the community of
its dreams. Our brothers are those whose childhood
was ruled by rhythms of the same epics and legends
as ours. We have all felt the coolness and the mist
of the morning of Austerlitz, and the emotion
of that long, sad evening when they first brought
the loaves of fern bread into a Versailles heavy with
silence. How many images white men need to give
themselves a national soul!

Reading and the theatre, for unsophisticated
people, are sources of imaginary lives. Nothing is
less disinterested than the desire to know. The West,
ignorant of opium, has the press. Each day's strug-
gling ambitions, defeated or victorious: a newspaper.
What a world swirls behind the eyes of an absent-
minded reader! This is what gives the men of our
race a walled existence. Nothing reverberates inside
them with the sound one would predict. Imagine,
my friend, that among us there is not a man who
has not conquered Europe. What possibilities for
scorn . . .

Have you a taste for the burlesque? Go to the
cinema. Its action enveloped in silence and its acceler-
ated tempo are perfectly suited to stir our imaginations. Observe the audience leaving when the film

is over: you will recognize in their mannerisms those of the characters they have just been watching. How heroically they go down the avenue! Hidden behind the foreheads of Europeans, my friend, are uncut phonograph records. Certain events, which affect our sensibilities strongly, engrave themselves there. Incited either by desire or idleness, the beast begins its tragicomic melody, a melody that will be only barely embellished by our culture, which at times will give us the comfortable feeling of being haunted by the ghosts of old mistresses . . .

It is a singular spectacle, this madness which contemplates itself. The fever for power great men have stirs us more than their acts—these are merely preparations for attaining a pose—and it gives them an attitude of detachment until an inopportune intervention of reality reveals their lack of harmony with it. Then who cares about Saint Helena, and what if Julien Sorel dies on the scaffold?

The young Frenchman, whom one hour of boredom has transformed into Napoleon, performs those deeds of the Emperor which have excited his imagination, but it is he who is the Emperor. The patterns of heroic lives direct him, controlling momentarily his docile imagination, which suddenly dominates them in its turn. At times an astounding clarity lends a hand to this madness: the imaginary general forms logical plans and pushes back fancied difficulties with methodical precision. The Western novel demonstrates clearly enough the power of the dream which demands from the intellect the means of making its madness believable.

We are not sketching a single illusory image of ourselves, but many images, some of which are

hardly even rough drafts that the annoyed mentality rejects, even though it collaborated on the
outlines. Any book, any conversation has the power
to make these images appear; reinvigorated by each
new passion, they change in accordance with our
most recent pleasures or latest pains. However, they
are potent enough to leave in us secret memories
which then grow so great as to constitute one of the
most important single elements of our lives: that
awareness we have of ourselves which is so veiled,
so opposed to reason that any attempt of the mind
to understand it only makes it disappear. Nothing
definite, nothing that allows us to define ourselves;
only a sort of latent power . . . As if we lacked only
the opportunity to carry out in the real world the
exploits of our dreams, we retain the confused impression, not of having accomplished them, but of
having been capable of accomplishing them. We are
aware of this power within us just as an athlete, without thinking about it, is conscious of his strength.
Pitiable actors who don't want to stop playing our
glorious roles, we are, in our own eyes, creatures in
whom is dormant an unsophisticated and jumbled
procession of the possibilities of act and dream.

In this kind of consciousness, sustained, with the
promises or hopes of human life, by all the riches
of delirium, being cannot lower itself to becoming:
being *someone*. This concept is beyond rational
discourse. And if we have never considered such
things, the reason is that Western meditations on
the subject have always accorded the "I" a state of
permanence. That it is distinct from the universe is
implicit in this position. The Chinese I have met do
not accept this duality at all, and I must admit that

it holds little sway over me. However hard I try to be conscious of myself, I sense only a chaotic series of sensations over which I have no command at all, and which are only dependent on my imagination and the responses it calls up. For dreaming, which is nonetheless action, is based upon a passive imagination made up of involuntary associations. The entire erotic game is there: being oneself *as well as the other,* feeling one's own sensations as well as imagining those of the partner. Sadism, masochism, even the feelings aroused by a play, all subject men to this division, final aspect of the ancient forces of fatality. A strange faculty, that of imagining sensations and experiencing them as well; stranger still, actually to understand such a game! For the mind now returns to be reckoned with: if, moved by these sensations, we react, it is the intellect which determines our reaction. Like discoveries, mistakes are also in its domain, for without the intellect forms disappear; and also in its domain is our common defense, the sense of the "I," suggestive of probabilities.

This defense against the unceasing entreaty of the universe is the mark of European genius, whether it expresses itself behind a Hellenic or a Christian mask. When a Catholic theologian calls the devil "Prince of the World," I think I hear the voice of ancient statues rising up out of the blackened bronze. The mark of our proud countries, as of a tribe, this voice, alternately exalted and despairing, crying its faith in the necessary limitations of man as his reason for being! Mark, also, of a race subject to the test of action, and thus destined to a most bloody fate.

9

Ling to A. D.

Cher Monsieur,

The distance between our sensibilities is in no way better illuminated than by the nature of our dreams. When we dream we do not consciously seek in our dreams the wisdom which life may have refused us . . . Wisdom; not glory. "The commotion of dreams," you wrote. I answer you, "The calm of dreams."

Yet the Chinese who dreams becomes wise. His dreams are devoid of images. He sees in them no conquered cities, no glory, no power, but the possibility of appreciating everything to the highest degree, of denying the ephemeral, and, if his soul is a little common, the possibility of some esteem.

Nothing inclines him to action. Even while dreaming . . . He *is*. To feel that he is respected is not to imagine that when he enters a room heads turn toward him. Rather, it is to know that in addition to the peculiarities of his personality, his stature includes the respect which he inspires in others. However strange this may seem to you, a Chinese imagines, if I may so express myself, without images. It is this which draws him to a quality rather than to a person, to wisdom rather than to an emperor. Thus the idea of a universe, of a universe which he cannot possibly conceive, corresponds, for him, to reality.

For a long time your race has sought to explain its existence. Carefully, you label, classify and limit other people, as well as yourselves. Armed with *pince-nez,* you go along, myopic and attentive, seeking shades of difference. The care which your sixteenth-century painters, for whom I feel some fondness, brought to their portraits—your minds have this same quality. Sometimes, when I am alone, leafing through one of the books you treasure highly, forgetting with the falling sun an anguish only too familiar these days, I take great delight in your hunt for the individual and in your efforts to hold on to such a precious captive. For, if you find yourselves, you do so in the manner of those magicians who, having called forth devils, discover their chambers invaded by numerous horned faces, and awaken late the next day under piles of books, suffering from terrible headaches. No, the books had not wounded them; but they remember how the devils contended fiercely among themselves, for each of them wanted to be the only true one; and this struggle only leads the ingenious sorcerers into new troubles.

We have always tried not to be seduced by an illusory shadow of ourselves. I note that the West now takes an interest in Buddhism, to which posture you ascribe an inexplicable importance. You really needn't worry yourselves about it at all. The masters of Buddhism have often attained a purity of discrimination and of intelligence which impresses me much more than your own, wherein I sense too much candid ardor. But they fall into the same errors as you. Seeking oneself and fleeing oneself are equally senseless activities. Whoever lets himself be ruled by the intellect cannot live except for it and by it. There is no more disastrous scepter.

We, on the other hand, do not wish to be conscious of ourselves as individuals. The work of our mind is to experience lucidly our fragmentary nature and to draw from that feeling a sense of the universe, not as your pedants reconstruct prehistoric animals with a few bones, but rather as we, merely by reading a name on a post card, evoke unknown countrysides striped by giant vines; for the supreme beauty of a cultured civilization is to be found in the careful avoidance of nurturing the "I."

Those notions of the universe you are unable to find in yourselves you replace with rational constructs. You desire a coherent universe. You create one, and draw from it, with great care, your own particular sensibility. But who can estimate how much it owes to your intellect? Our sensibility is greater than any of its specific concepts. The attitude which essentially distinguishes our geniuses from those of other lands has need neither of ethic nor aesthetic. For their sensibility, which tends only toward its own perfection, implies an aesthetic free of inner conflict. As for morality, it is senseless to try to separate it from art.

It is true that certain Westerners, in some of their books, have amused themselves in the attempt to reduce our thought to their own terms. But those who have really tried to understand it, those who, scornful of the symbols you are always seeking, actually came to us, quickly realized that the mind can be used for many purposes, and that the conquest of the world is much more desirable than the conquest of its order. They forgot, little by little, the teachings of Tuscan hills and French gardens . . .

I too have walked in your incomparable gardens where statues mingle their great shadows, royal or divine, with the rays of the setting sun. Their open hands seem to be raising a heavy offering of memories and glory. One's heart wants to discover, where the slowly lengthening shadows come together, a long-awaited law. Ah! what dirge will be worthy of a race which, in order to regain its greatest thoughts, only knows how to entreat its unfaithful dead? In spite of their terse power, European evenings are sad and empty, empty as a conqueror's soul. Among the most tragic and vain deeds of men, none ever seemed more tragic and more vain than your interrogation of all the illustrious ghosts of your race, so devoted to power, a desperate race . . .

How I need you now, delight of the conquered flesh in the overpowering night, inhuman thought suspended above the immense flame of the world, Asia . . .

10

Ling to A. D.

Cher Monsieur,

There is in us a capacity which you don't even realize might exist: an affinity for strange lives, lives
which are basically different from our own. It so
deeply impregnates our painting and sculpture that
these arts are incomprehensible to someone lacking a sound understanding of this capacity. The care
our painters take in observing their subjects cannot
explain the forms they finally set down; for we find,
in the allegorical images of gazelle and horse, for
example, the same emotion that affects us in paintings in which these animals, caught in motion, seem
to draw their charm from having been skillfully ob-
served.

The animals and the objects which you paint are
generally used to suggest a story. I am troubled by
this fact. It stems from that strange European illness,
the result of your overdevelopment of intellect, of
which I have already written. You have inquired,
without a smile, into the qualities and faults of animals, admired the loyalty of the dog and denounced
the hypocrisy of the cat. Formerly, in Europe, tribu-
nals were obliged to bring animals to trial and sentence them. This was a healthy practice, and I can't

tell you how much I regret that you have suppressed it. For therein I would find a symbol: I would admire, once again, that sense of order which distinguishes you from other races; I would be pleasantly amused by such a practice.

You are acquainted with the fable of the skull. When its author shows us the human head, forgotten at the side of the road, pursuing the traveler who defiled it, he is writing like a Western author. But when he makes us see, in the brightness of the frozen moon, this ball that rolls, jumps, bounds about and never stops annoying that terrified pedestrian, we feel that he supposes this head to be endowed with independent life, subject to its own being, and thus generically foreign to the human species. There begins the realm of the fantastic.

The vitality which penetrates our figures made you believe that our art delights in isolating the individual. Its source lies, in fact, in the abandonment of individual characters. The idea of species is for you quite abstract; it allows you to classify; it is a means toward knowledge. In us it is closely connected with our sensibility. The arts of Asia alone have created caricatures of animals . . . When I compare your art to our own, your sensations seem dispersed, ours almost as ordered as your ideas. Do you, a Christian, have any idea what a man can be when his sensibility is ordered?

When I say "cat" what dominates my mind is not a picture of a cat, but an impression of certain supple, silent *movements* peculiar to cats. You distinguish among species only by their outlines. Such a distinction applies only in death. (It is said that your painters used to study the proportions of the human body by sketching cadavers.)

The notion of species is an awareness of what ties together the forms existing in individuals who belong to a group: the necessity of particular movements. That is why it can no more be exactly defined than can style; but style can be achieved, the sense of species, only suggested. Suggestion is the highest technical perfection in art; it is the symbol of the living as the outline is the symbol of the dead. To understand a universe of successive existences one must first understand suggestion, and it is by suggestion that the artist, in his play, discovers the universe. It marks the profound distinction between your conquest and our own: you go from obvious analogies to more obscure ones, while we proceed to irreconcilable differences.

All afternoon I've been looking at paintings in the Louvre. To that unfortunate assemblage I prefer what the windows show me! This early spring which is passing through Paris enchants me. The quays of the Seine look like lithographs by your Romantic painters: they are at once glorious, charming and bourgeois; the palaces are surrounded by men selling birds. Your museums afford me no pleasure. The masters are closeted there; they are debating. That is not their job, nor is it ours to listen to them. And I am always depressed by those surroundings which show that you prefer the satisfaction of critical judgment to the finer joy of understanding.

A museum teaches only, alas! what foreigners expect of beauty. It compels one to compare, and above all to perceive in a new work the differences it communicates. It dominates the sensibility which offers itself to it; and I predict, not without bitterness, that my children's sensibility will undergo its dangers. Emotions, unexpected juxtapositions of colors, the aesthetic reveries which my grandfathers took from our canvases, all will rejoin, in death, the dreams which playthings inspire in children; they can only be distinguished in their quality . . . How many centuries of wisdom have advised us to make our imagination the continually new servant of our sensibility! Victorious over so many works of art, the tireless sadness of the West passes from gallery to gallery, while the young genius of the Seine makes a poplar-colored haze rise from the river . . . The countrysides of your land carry one, they say, to meditation; those of China dispose our souls toward joy or sadness. Certain of them, unfamiliar, are roused to sudden life by shadows on the snow or the red lines of a bridge; they become harmonious messages which speak to us of ourselves. Real or figurative, whether it arouses our sensibility or blends with it, a landscape is an ornate emotion. Those which we regulate—gardens—are almost traps. Indications of our feelings, they have great power over us, and changes in them trouble us profoundly. I recall one such garden which an ancestor of mine had laid out near Amoy, in the eighteenth century, by a well-known landscape gardener. My parents had chosen, to introduce me to it, one of those twilights at the close of summer which, in that region, are of extreme delicacy and make one aspire toward perfection. We arrived there late. The shadows had erased the contours of the ground; it seemed that the purity of the garden had remained for centuries unchanged.

Little by little a monastic peace had reclothed this place, to which it alone was suitable, as though to appease its wounded innocence. To the rhythm of the still warm wind the trees which our ancestors had loved, bending down and then slowly up again, seemed to balance, for a long moment, the landscape of low rocks, ponds and hills against the immutable marine horizon.

A belated sunbeam, almost without light but highly colored, which the sun shoots out before sinking to rest, crossed the trunks of the trees and suddenly lit up a part of the garden and, in the distance, several European villas which had not been visible until then. The disorder of the paths and shrubs and the presence of those foreign buildings so cruelly destroyed that calm beauty, heavy with the weight of the years, that I reflected on the shameful conclusion of a heroic life. Kingdom of fervor, whatever your ancient glory and nobility, there is one hour when the wound you carry in your heart cannot be hidden, and bleeds . . . That is the hour of deepest silence.

Unparalleled moment, time of unequaled solitude! In the agony of the goddesses gathered there, I found an emotion that I would never have dared demand of their glory. The blood which ran over their bodies destroyed them like flames, and adorned them as though with light . . . More even than their memory, I loved their murdered image. Their death attached me passionately to them, and the adolescent I was long remained drunk on the heavy perfume of their earthly blood . . .

11

Ling to A. D.

Cher Monsieur,

In this letter you will find the photograph of a mask of antique bronze. Someone sent it to me from China, and I send it back there to you. It is prior to the Han: two eyes and an engraved line indicating the nose. It evokes terror. It doesn't inspire it; it evokes it. The mouth, which in all Western primitive sculpture expresses emotion, is not even represented.

You know, as I do, the beauty of the images that Buddhism, troubled by Greece, carved on the flanks of our mountains. Despite the religious calm that falls from their closed eyes, profane as well as sacred China has not ceased for ten centuries to erase what there was of the human about them, to corrupt and transform them into objects of dreams and divine signs, gradually, with the force of the impassive sea. The figures on your cathedrals have disappeared in like manner. Here and there, as the thinning light of day scatters into stars, the vast perfection of a sovereign art bursts into a thousand precious bits. But this explosion, in China, is the result of a lucid but preposterous extension of dreams; in Europe, it is that of men, women, and their pleasures. You find yourselves standing on the empty pedestals of the statues of the wise; we find on them the symbols of wisdom, encircled by familiar monsters.

It is doubtless our use of ideographs that has prevented us from keeping ideas separate (as you have done) from that plastic quality which we always find in them. Our painting, when it is beautiful, neither imitates nor depicts: it signifies. A painted bird is a particular symbol of a bird, like its character the property of those who understand it and of the painter: bird is the public sign of the reality. Influenced by your art, I now see ours as the slow, precious conquest of dream and of emotion by the sign.

12

A. D. to Ling

etching. Our own art then seems to me that of another planet, and I console myself, deriving a complicated pleasure from doing so, with the great sadness generated in me by the knowledge that there is
no more art I cannot understand . . .

Europeans are weary of themselves, of their
crumbling individualism, of their exaltation. What
sustains them is less a thought than a delicate frame-
work of negation. Capable of action to the point of
self-sacrifice, but disgusted by the will to act which
today contorts their race, they would seek to discover
a more profound meaning in their actions. Their de-
fenses are disappearing one at a time. They are un-
willing to oppose the claims on their sensibility; they
can no longer do without understanding. This tendency, which drives them to abandon themselves, is
most present when they consider works of art. Art is
thus a most delicate pretext; the most subtle temptation is the one which we know is reserved for the
best of us. Today there is no imaginary world
which restless European artists do not strive to
conquer. An abandoned palace attacked by the
winter winds, the wall of intellect is gradually falling into ruin, and its crevices, which lend that charming, decorative effect, are widening. Yes, he who examines the art forms which have paraded through
Europe for the last ten years and doesn't want *to
strive* to understand them has an impression of a
kind of insanity, an insanity both self-conscious and
self-satisfied. These works, and the pleasure they
contain, can be "learned" like a foreign language;
but hidden in their rapid succession may be sensed
an agonizing force which dominates the mind. The

continual attempt to renew certain aspects of the universe by looking at them with new eyes is an effort involving an ardent ingenuity, which acts on man like a drug. These dreams, having once possessed us, call up still other dreams, in whatever way their magic exercises its power: through a plant, a painting, or a book. That special joy one takes in discovering unknown arts ceases with their discovery, and is then far from being transformed into love. Let there be other forms to move us, even if we will not love them, sick kings that we are, to whom each morning brings the most beautiful gifts of the realm, each evening returns that ever-present and desperate eagerness . . .

Our European malaise is caused, alas! by the discoveries of our most sophisticated minds.

Are you familiar with the *Conquest of New Spain*? In that old Spanish text, how Sahagun's voice seems to tremble gravely when he recounts that, on his arrival in Mexico, at the king's palace, he visited "gardens which were like nothing created by the hand of man, and, in the cellars, collections of snakes and sad dwarfs . . ." The sadness in the eyes of those West Indian dwarfs which troubled the Latin Father was recaptured by our civilization in our ancient art, in the marvels of Tuscany, then in that Louvre where the paintings, brought together by Napoleon, troubled, by their very number and variety, the artists who were most sure of themselves. But it is not Europe or the past which is invading France as this century begins, it is the world which is invading Europe with all its present and its past, its heap of offerings of living and dead forms, its meditations . . . This great, troubled drama which is beginning, dear friend, is one of the temptations of the West.

Should matter be victorious over mind there would be something more significant than the onslaught of pleasure and resultant exaltation of a slightly vulgar sensibility. Carnal pleasure and a taste for the new easily seduce mediocre minds, but would be powerless against someone who is ready for the struggle. Truly, a culture dies only of its own weakness. Faced with ideas it cannot absorb, it is condemned to find in their destruction an element of its own renaissance or its annihilation. Therefore, we are witnesses to the birth, in all of Europe, of the sometimes bitter play of artistic experiments. For everything can be tried by a culture whose elements are·bound together only as they are present in men. A few, profoundly aware that they are surrounded by extremely mobile objects and thoughts, place a higher value on the lucid contemplation of this unstable world than on the will to fix it. Also, it is only in the world that they can find their own countenance, about which they are curious. And further . . .

But nothing is more worthy of passion than their abrupt, violent and nervous attempts to recapture a lost quality. The Charioteer of Delphi, brooding Persephone, Romanesque Christs, Khmer or Saitic heads, bodhisattvas of the Wei and T'ang dynasties, primitives of all countries, these works are selected, first because they do not try to seduce, second because of the style, barely tinged with emotion, which they have in common and which we would call beauty. There lies the revenge of the intellect. The flood of living forms swells in it like a subterranean river, out of which it draws only those great and simple forms, even if they must later be carried off, to reign over others and submit them to their whims.

For this intellect, which refuses to grant judgment any true value, is led on by its own strength to be conscious of its need for a negative classicism, almost totally dependent on a horror of being seduced. The art it desires it conceives of less as the totality of a work than as an almost mathematical relationship between its parts. And it is less the satisfaction of a desire than the effort of a culture to ward off the incessant attacks of its enemies and of its own vitality, the most implacable foe.

13

Ling to A. D.

You, on the other hand, in order to express your concept precisely, are obliged to state that reincarnation concerns successive and different incarnations of a single soul. This distinction means nothing to us, who are unable to accept the quality of continuity which you attribute to that which you call "soul." We are incapable of placing several personalities in order, one following the other; we don't even know how to understand personality. The idea of individual existence was so undeveloped among us that, up to the time of the Revolution, parents were punished along with their children for crimes which the latter had committed without their parents' knowledge.

The successive forms of a soul evidence no relationship, unless one similar to that which exists between a cloud and the plant which is nourished by the rain. You know that nothing is aware of its previous states. It is difficult to delineate this idea with European words. Still, I can say that what has been translated as "You shall be reborn as a jackal" might be less inaccurately translated as "Out of your acts, when you die, a jackal will be born." This last is an attempt to express the thought of races for whom the jackal, not knowing he was once human, is subject only to animal laws; for whom the existence of destiny is not certified by an individual's awareness of it, but by the minute changes it brings to the world . . . Besides, what sense of the self can be found in a concept of destiny which is not based on the hopes of men? The concept escapes those who are not free from the thoughts and torments of men. The sages, who alone can conceive an absolute dominating our vain, terrestrial struggles, are conscious, not of individual destinies, but of a common

destiny. Here one finds the singular structure of
Eastern thought, at least as coherent as any Western
philosophy, but whose lines join only at infinity, as
in those gardens in Kashmir, where perspectives are
established when one looks through great open-
ings in the wall to the sky, to the distant, snow-cov-
ered mountains . . .

Your landscapes, on the other hand, don't upset
your idea of the dignity of man, which is so dear to
you. There is no spectacle of nature which you fail
to compare to some human work of art. The power
of mountains, which only calls up in you feelings of
calm grandeur, is incapable of giving you the sensation of an existence whose force is greater than
man's—like the disordered movements of vegetation
falling and rising again, dropping in a frothing ava-
lanche from the tops of peaks and, ever as densely,
plunging into the sea. This is not a divine force; on
the contrary, it is one of a more inhuman character,
incomprehensible, vegetable, a force which takes
hold of us only after we become aware of its existence.

Between Western and Eastern intellect I sense
above all a difference of direction, almost of aim.
The former desires to construct a plan of the universe and give it an intelligible form; that is, to establish between the unknown and the known a rela-
tion capable of bringing to light things which have
been obscure. It wants to subordinate the universe,
and finds in this desire a pride that becomes greater
the more intellect seems to dominate the universe.
Its cosmos is a coherent myth. The Eastern mind,
on the other hand, gives no value to man himself; it
contrives to find, in the flow of the universe, the

thoughts which permit it to break its human bonds. The first wants to bring the universe to man; the second offers man up to the universe . . .

Those who saw in the statues of the Temple of the Lamas only a parade of bizarre demons understood us no more erroneously than your scholars, before whose eyes the concept of the symbol has been lowered like a tapestry embroidered with magical patterns before the divinities of the temple. Life is the infinite domain of the possible. The idol of the many arms, the dance of death, these are not at all *allegories* of the perpetual flux of the universe. They are beings, impregnated with an inhuman life *which has made those arms necessary*. They should be contemplated as giant crustaceans brought up from the depths of the sea are contemplated. Both are disconcerting to us, show us suddenly how much simplicity there is in us, inspire in us the idea of an existence without ties to our own. But the former are only figures with weapons made of sand, while the others are superhuman intercessors.

The creation of divine figures is a sacred art. Prolonged meditation, a pure life, and the austerity of the monastery alone permit the artist to discover in himself a mystic emotion so powerful that it obliges him to give it a new form. This form, born of an anguished ecstasy, should not convey, to those who regard it, an idea, but rather a peculiar sense of disorganization, an emotion in the presence of one of the forces of the universe . . .

I use the word "emotion" intentionally. What prevents your understanding Eastern civilization is that for us the concepts of emotion and thought are not separate. Thought is tied to our way of life as love is to yours. Still, you believe you have numerous, discrete visions of experience, whereas you have only a mental disease which makes you think that this is so. You have discerned in men certain emotions and their most obvious causes; but you believe that there is, in what you call Man, something permanent, which does not exist. You are like highly serious scholars who, carefully noting the movements of fish, have yet to discover that fish live in water.

Confronted with a chaotic universe, what is the first requirement of the mind? To comprehend the universe. But we are unable to do this with the images it offers us, since we immediately realize how transitory they are; thus we try to assimilate its rhythm. Experiencing the universe is not the same as systematizing it, no more than experiencing love is the same as analyzing it. Only an intense awareness achieves understanding. Our thinking (when it is not occupied in dogmatic argument) is not, as is yours, the result of a body of knowledge, but is the equipment, the preparation for knowledge. You analyze what you have already felt; we think in order to feel.

For the Far-Eastern thinker there is only one kind of knowledge worth acquiring, that of the universe. He diligently tries to create in himself, according to established rules, states of thought and sensibility which are mutually continuous, which are directed, from their origin, toward a definite goal, and which succeed in giving intellectual insights, that is, hypotheses, a character of certainty.

The universe is the result of two opposing rhythms which pervade all existing things. Their absolute equilibrium would be nothingness, since all creation derives from a rupture of this equilibrium, and can only exist in diversity. These two rhythms are real only when their opposition is given human expression, whether it be in terms of masculine and feminine or of permanence and change.

We feel the same way about the universe as you do about your fatherland, and the types of sensibility thus determined are different only in this: our exaltation is not dependent upon a preference. Just as you give the patriotic emotion the protection of history, our thinkers have their own peculiar doctrines. The Taoists use rhythms in much the same way as you use rational constructions. In their manner, they learn to see in living forms only negligible things, born yesterday and already almost dead, like the succession of waves in ageless seas. Then, a peculiar method of breathing or, sometimes, contemplation of a mirror, makes them, after what is often a very long time, lose consciousness of the exterior world, and gives their sensibility an extreme intensity. The visual images which had been associated with contemplation, the origin of meditation, slowly disappear; they find in themselves only the concept of rhythm, which contains a powerful exaltation. When idea and exaltation are united, their rising intensity causes a loss of consciousness, which is the point of communion with their source, the unity of the rhythms being found only there.

14

A. D. to Ling

Mon cher ami,

Alas! all that seems highly arbitrary to me, as arbitrary as the worst system or the most false of our philosophies. I perceive the effort you have made not to separate, as we do, thought from matter, to derive from thought more than the poor, prideful joy it bestows upon us in the West. (Controlled breathing, against which Europeans who know you generally protest, hardly catches my attention. By itself, its only effects are those of low magic.) And I know that your emotions are, even more than ours, capable of attaching themselves to impersonal objects: you feel more tenderness for your ancestors, whether they are living or dead, than for your women. You use your education to confirm those of your emotions which depend on abstractions; and these abstractions allow you to observe your sensibility and recognize its sovereign power over you more clearly than women, gold, or domination would permit.

At the beginning of your quest I find an act of faith. Not as to the existence of this source, but in the value you assign it. In his ecstasy, the thinker does not identify himself with the absolute, as is

taught by your wise men; he merely defines as absolute the furthest point of his sensibility. The argument of your philosophers that all ecstasies are iden-
tical, since all begin where the material world ends,
seems invalid to me, and invalid the consequences
they draw from it. The only possible analogies are
with determinate things, as the indeterminate has no
analogue with itself, but is beyond the realm of anal-
ogy. Your description of ecstasy has to do only with
losing consciousness *in a certain fashion.* "To bind
oneself to the soul of the universe," they tell me, "is
to find consciousness itself." *"A* consciousness," I
want to reply, *"one* idea . . ." Even the most beautiful theorem of death is an answer only for weakness . . .

What engages me in all this is the importance at-
tributed to those emotions which are the property of the sensibility alone. Among your merchants,
among us Occidentals, I see men whose lives have
been determined by these emotions; and I suspect
that we are all at their mercy. I have been observing
China for almost two years now. What she has
changed in me most of all is the Western concept of
man. I can no longer conceive of Man apart from
his intensity. It is enough to read one psychological
treatise to realize how worthless our most penetrating general ideas become as soon as we want to use
them to understand our actions. Their value de-
creases as our search intensifies, and, always, we
hurl ourselves toward the incomprehensible, the absurd, that is, to the furthest point of the particular.

The key to this absurdity, is it not in the always
different degree of intensity that attends life? It is
felt by our voluntary, conscious mind as well as by

our more hidden existence, made up of dreams and secret thoughts spread out in absolute freedom. Whether a man dreams of being king or satisfied lover does not change his daily acts one whit; but let love, anger, a passion or a blow disable him: as the deeds of others resound in him with force or weakness, so will he be exalted or depressed . . . Werther embodies the proposition of death; nevertheless, it is only accepted by certain people at a given moment. And love, the love which must be differentiated from the desire to possess a woman, isn't it also a strange forest where, beneath our acts and our will, the sensibility plays and suffers as it pleases, and, at times, divides us, as if, *saturated by our emotions,* we could not bear them any longer? For our emotions are influenced more by their own existences than by external events. The inner life: a triumph of uncertainty; a mortal structure, singularly dangerous and ceaselessly renewing itself.

15

Ling to A. D.

Cher Monsieur,

Ah! who would think of denying that all that rests on what you call an act of faith? Such an act is arbitrary, you say. True. But what then allows you to live among other men and understand them? Whence comes your strength? And what awareness have you of reality, if not through compliance to such an act? Because you consider your civilization with a certain distrust, are you free of your dead, of your needs, and of that tragic danger which sleeps in the very heart of your life? My letter, moreover, only attempted to point out to you a possible direction, and its limits. The movements of the sensibility interested me when I was writing you, as well as several differences that should be noted, as is fitting, concerning the arbitrary nature of human existence.

My gradual acquaintance with Europeans compels me to write these words, and so does your letter, which provided the immediate occasion. The intensity which ideas produce in your race today seems to me to explain your life better than the ideas themselves do. For you, absolute reality was first God, then Man; but *Man is dead,* following God, and you search with anguish for something to which you can entrust his strange heritage. Your minor attempts to construct a moderate nihilism do not seem destined to long life . . .

What awareness can you have of this universe, on which you have based your unanimity, and which you call reality? The awareness of diversity. Total awareness of the universe is death—you have understood that fact. But your awareness of it is ordered and, consequently, mental. A poor prop, a mere reflection in the still water . . . The history of the psychological life of Europeans, of the new Europe, is a record of the invasion of the mind by emotions which are made chaotic by their conflicting intensities. The image of all these men dedicated to maintaining an idea of Man which allows them to overcome their thoughts and live, while the world over which this Man reigns becomes each day more foreign to them, is doubtless the final vision which I shall take away from the West.

16

A. D. to Ling

Mon cher ami,

I have seen Wang-Loh. For a long time he has in-
trigued me. But I was aware of his hatred for whites
and thus didn't want to look him up. The pose that
dates from his days in power, his almost secret pre-
cepts, the respect that surrounds him, all give the
impression of a profound and beautiful life. He
wanted to meet me; I was delighted.

He was staying at the Astor Hotel, and received
me in a very large room, done in the English style.
He is an old man, tall, clean-shaven, his hair
cropped close. His teeth are long, his jaw protruding,
his leanness such that his narrow eyes, behind the
protecting glasses, seem two large black spots, separated by his short nose. A death's-head wearing
tortoise-shell spectacles. An air of distinction.

At first, he questioned me. He was expecting certain remarks on the condition of Europe, in which
he has a malicious interest; then, concerning China:
"Never mind the savages with their sabers and the
indifferent millions who know only the fear of a
blow. Never mind the idiots intoxicated on university
nonsense. The condition of our best minds, simul-

taneously won over, yet disgusted by Europe, that's what counts today in China."

It was the third time I had sensed behind his words the notion that the aristocracy of intellect is alone worthy of consideration. On this point he is a true Chinese. Otherwise, the charm of his welcome, the finesse of which was by no means diminished by cordiality, his calm voice and antiquated gestures (he does not cut the nail on his little finger), give an impression of culture I haven't seen equaled in Europe. He seems to belong to a race quite different from those Chinese one observes gesticulating and shouting in the business quarters of commercial seaports. The secret of his charm and of his cogency undoubtedly lies in the contrast between the Western images in his visionary phrases and the calmness of his words, which his smile alone could contradict—that strange smile, neither joyful nor ironic.

"Our current play has a special power. The Theatre of Anguish. It's about the destruction, the annihilation of one of the greatest human systems, one which succeeds in existing without the support of gods or men. The annihilation! China wavers like an edifice on the point of collapse, and her anguish comes from neither uncertainty nor conflict, but from the weight of that trembling roof . . .

"With Confucianism in ruins, this whole land will be destroyed. All these men are dependent upon it. It created their sensibility, their thought, their will. It gave them a feeling of race. It formed the countenance of their happiness . . .

"The beginning of decline clearly delineates the nature of what is still standing. What have they been seeking during the last twenty-five hundred years? Man's complete assimilation of the universe; for their life has been a slow conquest of the universe, of which they wished to have their own fragmentary awareness. The perfection they drove themselves toward was unity with the forces of which they had become conscious, and also . . ."

I didn't understand the words which followed. I told him so. ". . . it is what is opposed to what you call individualism: disintegration, or, rather, the denial of all mental constructs, dominated by a desire to give everything, through the awareness one has of it, its highest quality . . . Such a thought carries the germ of its own illness—a contempt for power. China, in bygone days a minor adherent of power, seeks it again today, and brings to it, an offering to thankless gods, the intelligence of all her youth.

"The world will never recover the work of art that our sensibility once was. An aristocracy of culture and the search for wisdom and beauty are two faces of the same veiled demon . . . Watch their miserable debris fall to earth with the propaganda banners, from the Anfou Club to the least important political meetings . . .

"Those of us who are worthy of China's past are disappearing one by one. No one understands any more . . . Our tragedy is not in the bloody comedians who lead us, nor even in the constellation of death we see every night. If the Empire, with its russet plains, writhes like a wounded beast, what importance have these games of history?"

He still spoke slowly, without excitement, and was smiling.

"A more serious tragedy is unfolding here: our spirit is gradually becoming *empty* . . . Europe thinks she has conquered all these young men who now wear her garments. But they hate her. They are waiting for what the common people call her 'secrets': ways of defending themselves against her. Her effect on them falls short of seduction, and only succeeds in making them realize the senselessness of all thought.

"Unfortunately, we understand one another; we could never unite our indeterminate universe, which accepts infinity, with your world of allegories. The result of their confrontation is the supreme sovereignty of the arbitrary, a cruel and indifferent demon . . ."

He paused, hesitant. His gaze wandered to the light of the window and went blank. Silence. Then, alluding to the interest many young Asians have in Taoism, he continued in a lower tone:

"Ancient Chinese thought permeates their existence more than they think. The ardor which pushes them toward Taoism only tends to justify their desires, to give them greater strength . . . The intellectual uncertainty of the entire world brings them back to ancient doctrine: Buddhist modernism in Burma and Ceylon, Gandhism in India, neo-Catholicism in Europe, Taoism here . . . But Taoism, by showing them the existence of rhythms, by leading them to seek universal rhythms in the symbols of the Tao-Te-King, has alienated them from a flourishing culture because it added to man's constant striving the possibility of pleasure . . . There remains in them only the furious desire for destruction—wait and see. They are exasperated by a life and a thought which show only a common absurdity. Innovation, accumulations of money, territorial expansion, the construction of useless psychologies or allegories to interpret the universe, all that is vain, totally vain. We are incapable of becoming interested in ourselves, do you understand? Can you, a European, understand that? As for the dramas now unfolding both within us and before us, what can they bring other than disgust and misery? . . ."

He had stopped smiling. His body was bent toward me; his hands, at rest upon the table, trembled a little, and his voice, still slow, now had a sad overtone. But he continued. The smile returned to disturb his features. And as he escorted me to the door:

"The date of our national holiday—I wish it were not the anniversary of a revolution made by sick children, but of an evening when the intelligent soldiers of allied armies rushed out of the Summer Palace, carefully carrying the priceless mechanical trinkets which ten centuries had offered up to the Empire, crushing pearls underfoot and wiping their boots on the court robes of tributary kings . . ."

I turned when I reached the elevator. Framed by the doorway, his figure was etched in shadow. His hands had remained clasped, and, as they were still trembling, I thought I saw him, as I started down, render homage to the sadness he had just called forth with one of those brief salutes common to the rites of long ago.

17

Ling to A. D.

cinema, electricity, mirrors, phonographs, all have seduced us like new breeds of domestic animals. For the people of the cities, Europe will forever be only a mechanized fairyland.

But there is no China, only a few élite Chinese. The intellectual élite is no longer admired except as one would admire an ancient monument. The new élite, men who have absorbed Western culture, is so different from the former that we are obliged to think that a veritable conquest of the Empire by the West has begun. It is no longer her defeats, but her victories, which mark the destruction of China's past. And this destruction is irremediable, for a new aristocracy of intellect—the only aristocracy we have ever accepted—is forming: university students today have the prestige which was accorded formerly only to established men of letters, and feel themselves enveloped in that silent awe which used to surround these men. The existence of this new élite, the respect given it, represent a change in Chinese culture which heralds a complete transformation. The elders used to hold the highest rank in a society which was formed by and for them: candidates for important examinations were at least forty years old; today they are barely twenty-five. China is beginning to respect the value of youth, or, more accurately, its power. Well, totally giving ourselves over to youth will rapidly lead our civilization to chaos, just as the inexperience of young sailors smashes the sculptured prows of junks. The soul of this nascent China must be sought in the remnants of that old, magnificent structure which yet are vibrant enough to attract our youth. At least, when this culture we see getting weaker is almost extinct, it will retain the

sovereign beauty of dead cultures that calls forth
and adorns renaissances . . .

Wang-Loh's words are somewhat obscure. I don't
believe he deplores the disappearance of Confucianism, but of the possibilities for perfection that were
inherent in it. It had stirred in some men emotions of
great purity; such marvelous finesse, like the absolute of the Taoists, is attained by few. Confucianism, and especially its moral teaching, did not
develop from a religion and does not depend on one.
Christian morality is associated with certain deep
raptures in a Christian heart; Confucian morality is
basically social, and this accounts for its impact on
the social graces and faults of my race, as well as for
the tendency of my countrymen to be more conscious
of social relationships than of their own individuality. Such a morality, an aesthetic to cultivated minds,
an imperative to others, will not weigh on our con-
sciousnesses as the shadow of the cross weighs on
yours, but will soon seem a scattered sheaf of ancient laws.

What moved me most in your conversation were
the sentences in which Wang-Loh explained the
state of our intellect, wherein nothing that has been
destroyed has been replaced. I have myself experienced the anguish and disgust of Chinese confronted
with the acts of Europe, and I find these sentiments
in every letter I receive from China. Our young men
know that they need European culture, but they are
impregnated enough by their own to despise it. They
thought they could absorb it and still remain Chinese; a civilization which cares not for emotions nor
is moved by them could be learned, they thought,
as safely as a foreign language . . . Perhaps these

tortured beings, who today seem to be ruled by rancor and hatred while continuing to honor their heritage, will succeed in becoming part of some great Chinese thought or action. That in them which escapes the influence of the West ought to be enough to assure their Chinese identity . . . But these are European outpourings, a military bravura, an enthusiasm for the energy of young Cantonese, the love of women and the compassion of the new poetry of our North. Energy and love—empty . . .

How can I express the feelings of a disintegrating soul? All the letters I receive come from young men as desperate as Wang-Loh or myself, barren of their own culture, disgusted with yours . . . The individual is being born in them, and with him that strange, passionless desire for destruction and anarchy which would seem to be the highest form of amusement in times of uncertainty, if the need for escape were not the master of all these clenched hearts, if the pallor of great fires did not light them. If only you could see, as we Asiatics do, the long funeral procession of a dead Europe, with its white pallbearers leading Death's entire court! Biblical Magi, ambassadors of Mongol emperors, how poor and shabby your caravans! "I bring you, O Queen, all you could desire in order to die."

The desire to justify themselves that you find in all our social programs weakens them; but, behind all the proposed forms of government, behind all the quests for happiness that the tiresome irony of geniuses busies itself with, swells a force that soon no one will be able to conceal, and which will only make its appearance in arms: the will to destroy . . . Our miserable millions are conscious of injustice, not of justice; of suffering, not of happiness. Their disgust with their leaders only helps them understand what they have in common. I await with some curiosity the one who will come and cry to them that he demands vengeance, not justice. The power of a nation is greatly increased once it is based on the ethic of force. What then will be the acts of those who will accept the risk of death in the name of hate alone? A new China is being created which even we cannot understand. Will she be shaken by one of those great collective emotions which several times have convulsed her? More powerful than the chant of prophets, the deep voice of destruction is already heard in the most distant echoes of Asia . . .

The merchants buy and sell, and the River of Pearls reflects swollen stars in its calm sleep . . . What can I tell you? . . .

18

A. D. to Ling

Mon cher ami,

For the man who desires to live beyond his own immediate pursuits, a single conviction may organize the universe. But the worlds of fact, thought and deed in which we both live are not conducive to convictions; and our lagging hearts do not seem at all clever at enjoying, as they might, the disintegration of a Universe and a Man whose creation took the best efforts of so many minds.

Power escapes men twice: as soon as they have created it, again when they long to possess it. In the service of undirected energy, the elements of Western strength oppose and combat each other, despite provisional human contrivances; and the sense of order which they inadvertently give their universe escapes these men as it escapes readers of the news. Actions are dominated by their unforeseeable repercussions; the powers capable of changing facts become so rapidly loaded down with them that intelligence realizes that it cannot operate on any level of reality, that it cannot create the necessary unity between itself and the conviction which justifies it. It hardly bothers to distract itself by seizing the means of lying. But what matter the means when one is aware of their number and their potency? More or less distinct, the idea of the impossibility of grasping any reality whatsoever dominates Europe. The absolute power, even at its weakest, of a pope or a king today would be mere vanity; there is no longer a dominion great enough to influence consciousness. From this there follows a profound change in men, less important for the cries that proclaim it than for its breaking down of barriers which, for a thousand years, have enclosed and defended us from the outside world. What pleasure there is, my friend, for a troubled mind, in examining anarchic reality, the servant of energy, and which often makes the process of thought the means of becoming aware of inferiority!

Reality, when it declines, attaches itself to myths, preferring those born of the mind. What does this vision of uncontrollable forces evoke, as it slowly reconstitutes the old effigy of fate, in our civilization, whose magnificent, and perhaps fatal, law is that any temptation is dispelled by knowledge? . . .

At the core of Western civilization there is a hopeless contradiction, in whatever shape we discover it: that between man and what he has created. This conflict between the thinker and his thought, between the European and his civilization or his reality, between the indiscriminate consciousness and its expression in the everyday world through everyday means—I find it in every aspect of contemporary life. Sweeping away facts and, finally, itself, this spirit of contradiction trains our consciousness to give way and prepares us for the metallic realms of the absurd.

An effort at self-development, the only aim of

which is to acquire power, is not upheld by affirmation, but by a sort of opportunism, by a constant mobility, or by the acceptance of unilateral dogmas. Then too, since the weakening of the aristocracies of birth, the sense of caste has gained a strange hold on us. The desire to be distinct from others is not based on illusion alone; beside the fact that it is no longer within our ability to free ourselves from reality, we always tend to solicit reality whenever we consider it capable of giving us pleasure: it is the setting for our attempts at self-justification. Our esteem for caste, the result of our need for novelty, can easily be recognized in its special domain—the world of fashion, surely a better guide to the state of our soul than the sensibility you believe in. For fashion—by which I mean the changing styles in clothing, social attitudes, tastes or words—particularly in Europe and in the countries Europe has influenced, is the outward sign by which a provisional aristocracy, one in which the importance of social rank varies inversely with the time consumed in attaining such rank, attempts to establish itself. To assert oneself in the external world is to make oneself conspicuous—establish a difference between things of the same order. In our psychological life, our private world, it is to establish a difference in natures. The first of these impulses leads toward self-justification, the other toward realization of the utter uselessness of self-justification. They become more and more disunited and we are left with the perception of this separation. What irony in this two-pronged thought, in this introverted man who is permeated only by the discordant elements of the universe!

Some young men are becoming attached to the

transformation of the world which is taking place within them. It gives them a sense of uniqueness which their mentality needs in order to survive. The mind becomes the servant of change, and has no other function than to point out to them the mobility of an unstable world, a world forced to accommodate itself, like a trained animal, to any feeling, action, or thought, according to unknown patterns that thus become clear. For thought, when it becomes its own object, is more at odds with the universe than passion is. A man who takes another's life, or who commits other more secret deeds of which the law is ignorant, might find himself burdened by his crime itself, *or* by the new universe it imposes on him. Some strange faces are reflected in the mirror which is war. Is it we who are changing, or is it the world, when passion withdraws, like the sea, from the passionate act which alienated us from that world?

Even more than that of the young Chinese about whom Wang-Loh spoke, our thought is falling in ruins . . . With calm distress we are becoming conscious of the profound opposition between our acts and our inner lives. The intensity of the latter cannot belong to the mind; sensing this, the mind revolves emptily, beautiful machine soiled by bloodstains . . . For this inner life is also the most primitive, and its power, which exhibits the arbitrariness of the intellect, cannot save us from mind, to which it says, "You are a lie, the very means of lying, creator of realities . . ." And the mind answers, "True. But always, when the day ended, men thought they saw rich prizes in the darkness, and the riches you offer are only the last reflections of the dying daylight."

In order to destroy God, and after having destroyed Him, Western intellect has abolished all which might have stood in the path of Man: having reached the limit of its efforts, it finds only death, like Rancé before the corpse of his mistress. It discovers that it can no longer be enamored of the vision it has at last achieved. Never has there been as disquieting a discovery . . .

There is no ideal to which we can sacrifice ourselves, for all we know is lies, we who have no idea what truth is. The earthly shadow which falls behind marble gods is enough to keep us from them. How firmly man is bound to himself! Fatherland, justice, grandeur, truth—which of his statues does not carry such trace of human hands as would evoke in us the same ironic sadness as old and once-loved faces? But the effort to understand doesn't permit every folly. And yet what sacrifices, what injustifiable acts of courage are dormant in us . . .

Of course, there is a higher faith; the one offered by all the village crosses, and by the very crosses which watch over our dead. That faith is love, and brings peace. But I shall never accept it; I refuse to lower myself by requesting the peace my weakness cries out for. Europe, great cemetery where only dead conquerors sleep, whose sadness is deepened by the pride taken in their illustrious names—you leave me with only a naked horizon and the mirror of solitude's old master, despair. Perhaps he also will die of his own existence. From the distance, in the port, a siren howls like a dog off its leash. Sounds of vanquished cowardice . . . I am contemplating my image. I shall never forget it.

Unstable image of myself, I love you not at all.

Like a deep wound, badly healed, you are my dead glory and my living pain. I have given you everything, and still I know that I shall never love you. Without bowing down, each day I shall bring you peace as an offering. Voracious lucidity, I still burn before your tall and solitary flame in this heavy night, while the yellow wind cries, as in all those foreign nights when the wide wind echoed around me the proud outcry of the sterile sea . . .

1921-1925